BECOMING
THE BANK

I would like to thank Karen Sucra. Her dedication at the start of this project was paramount to getting it completed.

IQlend.ca

ISBN: 978-1-7780442-0-5 (print)
ISBN: 978-1-7780442-1-2 (ebook)

Ordering Information:
Special discounts are available on quantity purchases by corporations, associations, and others. For details, visit becomingthebankbook.com.

CONTENTS

BECOMING THE BANK

The Simple Lending Process that Creates
Passive Income for Everyday People

CHAD ROBINSON

INTRODUCTION: DOUBLING YOUR MONEY!

Are you looking for a way to take control of your investment portfolio and set the terms of your investments while reaping higher overall returns? Let's not kid ourselves—WHO ISN'T? Have we got your undivided attention? Odds are that you are at least curious to see what this untapped and potentially lucrative opportunity may be. The wealthy have been doing this for years, and it is the second oldest profession in the world: lending money.

Chances are if you are picking up this book, you want to earn high returns with low risk. You work hard for your money—it should work equally as hard for you. The "establishment" wants you to think that lending money is complicated. Don't despair; it isn't. This book will fill the information-gap that surrounds a growing investment opportunity within the mortgage sector—the often untapped world of **private lending**.

It can't be overstated that the financial sphere and, in particular, the mortgage sector is full of books on different topics pertaining to the often somewhat mysterious field of mortgages and real estate. So many questions to answer. So many areas to cover. However, there are a couple of inherent problems.

First, there is too much information about general real estate and mortgage issues and next to no information on specific areas that can be explored for investment purposes. Don't you hate that? There are so many books and seminars promising to teach you how to become a millionaire, but at the end they still leave you wondering, "Yes, but how?"

Second, there is no single book that completely covers the nuts and bolts of private lending. It is not the quantity of the information that is out there, but rather the quality and how in depth the material is. This is about to change. Finally, you have picked up a book that is devoted entirely to the specific and potentially highly lucrative field of private lending.

Let's not sidestep the obvious questions. The question that is probably at the top of your list when you open this book is, "Why write a book about private lending?" You're probably also wondering, "Just what is private lending?" "What will I get out of becoming informed on the topic?" "How will this translate to an increase in income for me?" and "Is this a viable and sustainable area to be actively involved in?"

These are common questions. You can and you will benefit from an insider's look into this often misunderstood area of the real estate sector. Too many people are put off from exploring the fascinating area in depth because either they feel they do not know enough, or worse, they are given the wrong information that has the potential to set a would-be private lender on the wrong footing.

We will learn about the magic of transferring your investments into a self-directed Registered Retirement Savings Plan (RRSP) that will give you the control over how much money you lend out as well as setting the terms of the private mortgage loan. All without the interference and hefty charges imposed by the big banks!

We will also touch upon the benefits of lending out from Tax-Free Savings Accounts (TFSAs) and other registered accounts that will give you the added advantage of compounding interest and tax-free withdrawals!

These and other pressing issues pertaining to the art of private lending will be explored. Don't be intimidated. Mortgages and private lending can be fun and can certainly be broken down for you to make it more than clear. Join me on a journey toward becoming a private lender. You will not regret it, and your bank account will thank you, too.

My Story

This book has been swimming around in my head for quite some time. It started as a side project and grew into a full-blown course geared toward the principals of private lending. Now it is time to put all my experience, firsthand examples, and a basket full of ideas into print—written in a way to both entertain and educate you.

This is the way my mind works. I have many projects on the go, properties to manage, several businesses to run, and a wealth of information that needs to be expressed. One thing is for certain: private lending is a niche market and untapped in many ways, so I will take the lead and steer you through it. Given today's volatile world and stock market, a simple, stable investment is needed now more than ever. Real estate in its most fundamental form is easily understood. I will teach you how to lend on the hard assets and SECURE your investment.

Who am I, really? Well, on paper, I am a father of four and a devoted husband. I am also an entrepreneur and a real estate professional. I am the owner of several thriving businesses, in addition to being a licensed real estate broker and mortgage broker.

I have written and contributed to several real estate magazines, and I have served as a talking head on mortgage issues at conferences and trade journals. I give courses and presentations on becoming a successful private lender as well as other topics relevant in today's mortgage market at investor conferences.

This may be what I do, and indeed what pulls me in a million different directions, but who am I really? What makes me tick? I can tell you that, at heart, I am both a family man and a lifelong entrepreneur. I simply think outside the box and take the risk and necessary steps to take a great idea and transform it into a successful business venture—the same thinking that is required to be a successful private lender.

Now I don't want you to jump to the conclusion that private lending must be a risky endeavour. I can assure you that if you are going to dive into the world of investments, investing in real estate is by far the one least risky form of investment. You will see this clearly as you read the upcoming chapters.

Yes, like most of you, my family comes first, but I am always planning. Every day I wake up and get breakfast on the table for my kids, drive them to school and after school activities, all while my mind is working on how to improve my current businesses and conceptualize new business ventures. I am thinking ahead. I am looking at the different avenues open to me and creating plans to maximize the best possible outcomes.

I will argue throughout this book that this way of thinking is very necessary in order to truly profit in the exciting field of private lending, or any investing for that matter. It gives you the ability to recognize a potentially profitable private mortgage investment opportunity and then have the necessary components in place to take advantage. It is helpful both in terms of how we view a deal as well as taking the steps we know we have to take to negotiate a deal with a prospective borrower.

I bring up this "mindset" that I have practised for so long in my career at length in this book, and it will suit you well as you go forward in your private lending journey. Mindset truly does equal success. That's another of my many mottoes!

I am convinced that in order to be successful at something you have to have a passion for it and be willing to take some degree of risk to make things happen. I'm sure you have many ideas circling in your head. Some of them are very good ideas that given the right planning could translate into potentially profitable business ventures.

The problem is that very few of us are willing to see our ideas transform from concept through to fruition. The element that is missing is the ability to believe in the concept and take the steps necessary to build that concept into a thriving business. The road to building a business has not been without the element of surprise and certainly can be humorous at times.

Thinking outside the box and being willing to take a financial leap are obvious and necessary components to becoming a profitable private lender. I knew I had it in me from a very early age. At age 12, when other kids my age were playing soccer in the schoolyard, I was organizing friends to help me build my lawn maintenance business. I had more fun and fulfillment out of taking this idea and translating it into a profitable business venture than scoring a goal on the soccer field. Not to mention I wasn't very good at soccer.

My entrepreneurial spirit has taken me far and guides me through all areas of the mortgage and real estate industry, not to mention a few dabbles into the software world. This spirit, along with courage to take those risks, are the keys to success in private lending. Let me remind you once again that the risk that we are referring to here is minimal compared to taking your chances on the volatile stock market. What does real estate almost always do? **It is almost always appreciating.** It gains in value. Any money you invest will more than likely see a noticeable return. Unlike many other investment opportunities, lending in mortgages allows you to have a SECURED position on the actual house or property. Yes, just like the banks. There is a reason the banks make billions of dollars; mortgages are one of those reasons.

Now that I have your attention and you are armed with the attributes that will turn private lending into a profitable pursuit, we have to figure out just what exactly private lending is.

All you need is the plan, a road map, and the courage
to press on to your destination.

– Earl Nightingale

CHAPTER 1: SO, WHAT EXACTLY IS PRIVATE LENDING?

I obtained my real estate licence before I turned 20. It was logical. I was literally born into a real estate family. My mom still works as a successful realtor today, well into her 70s. It is quite simply in my DNA. My family often jokes that I was born while my mom was writing up an offer on a property. At that time, writing an offer was not as easy as it is today. It required actual typewriters and carbon paper sheets that you put between paper when you typed to create duplicates.

I knew what I wanted to do and what I wanted to achieve. I set the parameters that enabled me to work toward success in this fascinating industry. Set the goals, envision your end result, and put in place the road map to drive your route to success. This is my motto—a motto that you will see in later chapters that will also serve you well as you embark on your new career or side endeavour as a private lender.

As I was looking forward to my future career goals upon graduation with a BA in economics, it soon became abundantly clear that I would continue to be most successful in the area that truly drives me. This brings me back to the concept of passion. Real estate and everything to do with it has motivated me from early on and remains my career focus.

Over the years, after financing and coaching many small builders, I have moved into the realm of real estate development, buy and hold investment, and of course private lending. Is my enthusiasm rubbing off on you yet? I am hoping that my enthusiasm has not diminished over the years in this ever-changing industry and will inspire you to take the leap toward becoming a private lender and investing in real estate with confidence and excitement.

Now, if becoming a private lender, or at the very least learning about this area of real estate, is becoming appealing (how could it not be after having a taste of my story and chutzpah for the field?), we still have yet to answer the question of most relevance: How do you define private lending?

Simply put, private lending is the process of lending money to a third party via different potential avenues. You basically become the bank or lender. In private lending, and indeed as a private lender, there are different lending sources available to you. For example, you can lend cash, home equity line of credits (HELOCs), Registered Retirement Savings Plans (RRSPs), Retirement Income Funds (RIFs), and Tax-Free Savings Accounts (TFSAs), just to name a few.

It is more than likely that if you are considering privately lending out your funds then you have already tried different investment strategies and options in the past. You will more than likely also have money invested in any number of pre-existing investment vehicles. Essentially, you can lend out money from any investment vehicle that you have parked your hard-earned money into.

It is entirely up to you. You will see that I have a preference for investing a particular investment vehicle. I'll get into this later in the book. Suffice it to say there are investment vehicles that are perfectly suited to investing your funds privately for mortgage. I have devoted Chapter 13 to the obvious advantages of tapping into your self-directed RRSPs and other registered accounts.

The big takeaway here is that you are in the driver's seat when it comes to deciding what funds you want to lend out. This highlights the biggest advantage that you will experience as a private lender. As you can see, there are multiple platforms in which you can lend out to a third party, which allows for flexibility in loan options for a potential private investor.

If you are reading this book, chances are you already have an interest in real estate. Maybe you have been sitting on some money and are searching for a potentially lucrative method to invest (that does not involve playing with the stock market). It cannot be stated strongly enough that there are many ways to invest your money.

As I mentioned earlier, thinking creatively and outside the box pays dividends. You may have been relying primarily on retirement savings options or put a majority of your hard-earned cash into the often volatile stock market. Now you are looking for other options.

Many people can earn a lot of money in the stock market and other investment vehicles. I was having a conversation with my teenage son the other day about the stock market. His favourite store, GameStop, has just had an incredible stock run. It went from $19 to well over $300 in a matter of weeks. Why? The stock price was run up by investors who put their money into the company even though it was on the verge of bankruptcy. When I was in university, we learned how to value companies based on income and assets—you know, those pesky things called financial statements. Well, I stopped investing in stocks years ago when the market no longer cared. Many people who invest in stocks don't even know what a balance sheet is. Scary stuff. Logic has left the building. This led me to investment in something I can drive by. Something I can touch. Something that I can sell. Real estate and mortgages.

When you decide to become a private lender (and I am certain my encouragement and downright excitement about the topic is starting to pique your curiosity) you are lending your funds directly to the third party. You are probably thinking, "This is too risky to wrap my mind around! What if I don't see my money again! What, if any, sort of return will I get in the realm of private lending?" Don't sweat it.

The key here is that the security in question *is* real estate. You secure your investment via a mortgage on the title of the real estate, whether it be a house, building, new construction, or land. Sometimes we can secure our investment on things other than real estate such as boats, trailers, cars, or even motorcycles. Look at these other means of securing your investment as secondary sources, or as we like to say in the real estate biz, sweeteners. A little more sugar in your coffee or a little extra to seal the deal.

Obviously, I have always looked at investments from a real estate perspective. The question that I have to ask myself is, "Can I sell this property?" This is the bottom line. This is the question that is foremost in my mind when looking at a potential private lending arrangement. Why? Because a mortgage is an investment and "the property" is our security.

Ask yourself other pertinent questions. How much am I willing to put in? With any world event, be it a health scare, oil interests, or an upcoming election of importance, the stock market will feel the effects. So too will the money that you invested in it!

All of these questions lead back to the most obvious and important question: Will this property sell, and at what price? You will be asking yourself all these questions as you lay the groundwork and prepare to be a private lender. These questions are worth reviewing to further hone your skills as an existing private lender.

So, if you have money invested in a Registered Retirement Savings Plan (RRSP) or a Tax-Free Savings Account (TFSA), ask yourself: can I be using this money to lend directly to a third party? I can tell you that the rate of return on a mortgage deal will represent more than what most combinations of funds will provide sitting in a TFSA. You must be willing to take the financial leap.

I am going to mention three major points that will become clearer to you as you read on.

1. What I love most about private lending is that it essentially boils down to **my Private Pricing Matrix. For your free excel version please visit** becomingthebankbook.com.

Credit	Loan-to-value			
	<65%	65%-75%	75%-85%	85+
A	BR - 1%	BR -0	BR +1%	BR + 3%
B	BR	BR +1%	BR +2%	n/a
C	BR + 1	Br + 2%	BR +4%	n/a

Example Base Rates (BR)	
1st Mortgage	7%
2nd Mortgage	10%

Adjustments	
Self-Employed	Add 2%
Current Default	Add 4%
Land	Add 2%
Construction	Add 4%
Unique Feature	Add 1%
Blanket Mortgage	Add 1%

In other words, the interest rate is determined by the merits of the deal. (If this is not clear, it will become more so as you progress through the book.) Suffice it to say, you will be able to determine your own comfort level when it comes to the mortgage loan you want to structure. Each mortgage loan will have its merits. It is up to you to determine what your goals are when deciding which mortgage loan to negotiate.

Again, my objective here is not to have you running for the hills in a panic when you hear the word "risk." Rather, know that the risk level will always be low compared to other forms of investments.

On the most conservative end of the spectrum, you leave your money in a bank account. Here you earn effectively zero percent. Some would say even -2 percent when you factor in inflation. However, it is very secure. It is backed by the government and the banks. On the other end of the spectrum is investing in emerging markets, initial public offerings (IPOs), hedge funds, options, futures, and penny stocks. Let's put cryptocurrency, like Bitcoin, in the mix for fun as well. Mortgages are on the low end of the risk spectrum. It's not something you will brag about at dinner parties, but mortgages bring a quite slow and steady return that will make you very happy in the long run.

It is important to know that there are different types of mortgages and loans that you can explore and ultimately structure with the right borrower. Each loan has a fairly predictable interest rate range that you can attach to it, and by the same token it has a fairly predictable level of risk associated with it.

For example, a first mortgage will allow you to charge a 6 to 8 percent interest rate to your borrower with low risk. A second mortgage will provide you with more opportunity to charge a higher interest rate of between 10 and 18 percent, or higher. The risk associated with this type of mortgage is slightly higher, but so is the reward—higher interest payments.

If you are thinking that you may consider lending out money toward a third mortgage, for example, then the risk is more than for a first or second mortgage loan. Having said that, the potential to make a greater profit goes up in relation to the risk you have taken.

2. Next, as a direct private lender you have full control.

- You have control over setting the interest rate.
- You have control over where you lend.
- You have control over whom you lend to and of course how you lend your money.
- You have control over the terms of the loan.
- You have control over what type of loan you will negotiate (unlike many other types of investments where a "manager" chooses all those things for you).

With this level of choice and control, you truly are moulding your mortgage deal with a potential borrower. You are crafting a deal by deciding the terms you will be setting based on your comfort level and how you want to fashion your mortgage deal.

You call the shots. Where else in life do we have this luxury? Certainly not on the home front! The kids took over years ago. Let's not fool ourselves! You are at the dance and decide which partner you will choose. How can this not be an attractive alternative to the often restrictive platforms that are available for investment purposes?

Remember the banks have mastered the art of setting the terms they see fit for decades. You could learn quite a bit from how the banks think when lending out money. They have mastered the art of loaning out as little as possible for the highest interest rate they can and with as little risk to their bottom line.

I can tell you that the banks do not want you to know about the lucrative area of private mortgage loans. Why? Well, if you decide to lend out money from your self-directed RRSP (which I will go over in depth later), the bank will not be earning any commission on this financial transaction. From the bank's perspective, why would they suggest that you use your financial sources for this purpose? We know better! It is now your turn to be your own private bank.

Does the stock market provide you with this level of control over the terms of your investments? You can choose a stock or a mutual fund, but does anyone really know how those things work anymore? There is so much auto-trading going on computers making buy and sell decisions that wipe out tens of millions of dollars in the blink of an eye. Private debt may be the last bastion of common-sense lending.

I will also go over managed services in this book. Like property management for real estate, there are alternate forms of investing in private mortgages. More on that later.

3. Private lending provides an investor flexibility. This degree of flexibility obviously pertains to the overall level of control that you possess as a private lender. You have the flexibility to decide:

- What type of loan you will structure (blanket mortgage, first mortgage, second mortgage, third mortgage, bridge loan, new construction loan).
- What terms for the loan work best for you. You have a good deal of flexibility to determine the terms of your loan with your borrower including the length, type, interest rates, penalties, etc.
- Who you want to lend your funds to (your prospective borrower).
- How you find your prospective borrowers (mortgage professionals, networking, professionals).
- The type of interest arrangements you may prefer (delayed payment interest strategy, stepped up interest, or deferred interest).

Along with the overall control and flexibility that you have as a private lender there are other advantages as well when compared to other forms of investing:

- You will not be reliant on the ups and downs of the financial markets. Real estate investment is a separate form of investment and is generally safe from this volatility.
- If you are looking for reliability and level investment strategies, real estate is a very good option.
- There is great potential for making a profit since you can—in some of the higher loan-to-value deals—easily assign double-digit interest rates, which will set you up nicely for seeing very good returns on your investments.
- All the fees that are associated with structuring the mortgage deal can be assigned to the borrower to cover. As well as a private lender, you will not have to face any commissions on your investments or pay various fees to a financial adviser or institution.

> The borrower had a major family illness and got behind on his mortgage payment. He owed $250,000 to a large bank on a home valued $800,000 in a major city. He ignored all the letters and phone calls, until the sheriff came. At this point, he reached out to a mortgage broker, and we ended up lending $300,000. Enough to pay out the mortgage, all fees, all debts, and included a year's worth of payments. Rate of interest was 10 percent for two years.

What About High-Profile Lending Deals Gone Wrong?

Part of the reason I wanted to write this book is that there is a fear that has surfaced in the general public surrounding real estate investments and what could go wrong. Some of this fear is based on lack of true knowledge about the field of private lending, while other fears are based on what some people have heard.

Since the financial crisis of 2007–2008, the media has focused a considerable amount of attention on real estate deals gone wrong. They've often covered lenders and investors being misled by less-than-honourable mortgage brokers and suffering financial losses as a result. The 2008 financial crisis had its roots in very complex Wall Street shenanigans. In essence, there was so much money flowing around that Wall Street bankers created some very complex mortgage products that few people understood. This resulted in borrowers being able to get financing they should never have had in the first place. Many of these loans where called NINJA loans. NINJA stood for No Income, No JOB, NO ASSETS! They would actually give people 105 percent or 110 percent financing on a home when they had no income or any means of repayment. It is my hope that after reading this book, you will learn how to invest wisely and spot these types of high leverage, high-risk deals.

The media always love to go the negative. So yes, there have been cases where investors have been taken advantage of and misled. In any industry there is the potential for bad apples. There is also the potential for a bad deal as a result of the misguided intentions of a few. The real estate and mortgage industry is not immune just as other industries have the same potential for misconduct.

The actions of a few should have no bearing on what you will want to achieve as a private lender. You must be aware that a very small minority may try to take advantage of the system. With the knowledge you will gain from this book and carefully researching your mortgage deals you should be able to carve out a rewarding career as a private lender or lucrative past time.

Regarding the sporadic real estate deals that went south, it is clear that what is essentially at play here is the **lack of concrete information available to help educate private lenders**. Being able to recognize a potentially bad deal and having the insight and information to only invest in sound property investments is paramount to forging a lucrative and satisfying private lending career. I am determined to provide what is needed to equip you with the skills and knowledge to invest safely and at low risk to you.

Most people can understand a real estate deal and a simple mortgage—especially after reading this book—versus the complex options in the stock market that even "experts" don't really fully understand. The train for stock pricing being priced based on fundamental analysis left the station long ago. Don't worry about missing that train. Hopping on board the private lending train is a far more straightforward journey and more relaxed!

When considering an investment there are three basic questions you must ask yourself and answer yes to:

1. Do I understand it?

2. What is my security? In my opinion, only registered first and second mortgages count.

3. Do I understand the asset (i.e., the security)?

Big Banks Have Been Doing It for Decades!

Let's talk about traditional forms of lending. By "traditional," I mean big banks and what terms they rely on to loan out money for anything from an owner-occupied property to a new build, commercial construction, or land deal. Be clear that the banks are working within strict parameters. Loans through these institutions are based primarily on credit scores and income and other numbers to reach a set threshold that is considered to be low-risk lending in the eyes of the bank.

Where does this put the individuals who have the capital or means to buy a house but do not meet the strict criteria set out by the traditional lenders (big banks)? Over the years, I have been approached by potential clients that did not fit the mould of the big banks but were in need of access to cash quickly. I can assure you that the demand is out there. Having clients like these encouraged me to lend privately more and more. As in any other area of the economy, the market dictates the need. Right now, the number of clients choosing to go through non-traditional channels and borrow privately is increasing.

You may be wondering if private lending is the same thing as the other terms you have probably heard flung around. Maybe you heard the term hard money lending or hard money loans. This term is used frequently in American books geared toward private lending or other platforms such as American financial blogs.

The term "hard money lending" in America is essentially the same thing as private lending. In Canada, however, there are regulations put in place provincially pertaining to the area of private lending. Our rules are very different in Canada. As I mentioned earlier, just being versed in the correct terminology will put you on good footing. Knowledge and understanding of this burgeoning industry will help you to avoid some of the pitfalls that have occurred with private lending.

At the risk of sounding too much like an Economics 101 lecture, I have to define two things at this point to help us build the framework for the area of private lending.

1. **Debt:** Simply put, this is a loan with interest. Examples include credit card debt, mortgages, any personal or business loan, or a car loan. You get the idea. I am sure you were hoping to have had that credit card debt paid off by now!

2. **Equity**: Simply put, this is ownership with profit sharing. Examples include stocks, or anything sold publicly, like the New York Stock Exchange or shares in a company.

Why is it so important to understand the definition of these two terms and what they really represent? The answer lies in what we touched upon earlier. The notion of safety. What people often intrinsically feel is risky is actually a sound investment and a real opportunity to see a healthy financial return. This will become more than clear. Trust me.

Believe it or not, there is such a thing as "good debt." What? Doesn't this go against common sense? As in life, not every debt is created equal! If you look at it from a strictly money-making perspective, then one of my favourite authors—and a man who gives out no-nonsense financial advice—states it in a way that I feel best outlines my point.

David Chilton wrote a book decades ago that has become a financial cult classic: *The Wealthy Barber*. It's a classic because the advice given stands the test of time and applies perfectly to the field of private lending. He also wanted to differentiate between bad debt and good debt. Such an important distinction.

Just to digress here for a moment, I am still thrilled today that I have an autographed copy of the sequel in my bookshelf—*The Wealthy Barber Returns*. I always have room in my life for no-nonsense financial wisdom. In his sequel, Chilton calls good debt, and by this we can safely say real estate in any form is, "Money borrowed to buy an appreciating asset."

The key word, of course, to take away from Chilton's definition of good debt is *appreciating*. You will see a return on your investment as a private lender because you are dealing with an asset that will generally appreciate. Your investment is secured on, and based on, this guiding principal and financial reality. Often yielding a larger return then you will ever reliably see in other means of investment mentioned earlier in this chapter.

The bigger the risk, the higher the return. Real estate will see a return—sometimes huge returns if you lend out to clients in hot markets like West Vancouver or certain neighbourhoods in growing cities! So, a mortgage, which is technically a debt when we use financial terms to describe it, is in actuality a debt that you want to have. This debt will be making you money!

Given the fact that I know that you are a savvy investor—otherwise you wouldn't be reading this book—I don't need to point out various forms of bad debt. Car loans, for example. Have you ever seen a car appreciate? Just drive it off the lot and you will see 10 percent of the value evaporate. Poof!

Obviously, credit card debt, overextended lines of credit, and personal loans are not debt you want to carry for long. Really, all you have to do is just have a look at your Mastercard statement at the end of the month to figure that one out!

You know that some credit cards and some lines of credit have interest rates hovering around 18 to 20 percent attached to them. This is interest that you will have to pay back to the financial institution plus the principal amount. It's obviously a bad debt in the financial sense. Wouldn't you rather lend out money (a debt, technically) and be able to charge interest rates that can be as high as around the 28 percent range for a typical third mortgage?

Don't be scared of second mortgages. Sometimes people lend borrowers a second mortgage at 12 to 14 percent interest to pay off high-priced interest of credit cards at 20 percent or more. At first this many seem risky, or you may not understand why this is advantageous to the borrower. Take a look at the example below.

Sylvie was a part-time nurse, and her husband was a labourer. They had a nice single home in Milton, Ontario. For various reasons, they accumulated a fair bit of credit debt, and they could not get ahead of it. This client was looking to consolidate their debt by refinancing their single-family home.

> Income: $95,000
> Occupation: Labourer and part-time nurse
> Location: Milton, Ontario
> Property Type: Single-family home
> Amount: $140,000
> Beacon: 565/520
> Rate: 9.95%
> LTV: 80%
> Fee: 3.00%
> Position: 2nd
> Term: One year

Combined, the couple had over $95,000 worth of debt, their credit score was under 600, and they had a high debt-service ratio. This also caused their credit score to drop significantly. This resulted in a consolidation of the credit card debt to save the client over $900 a month! One year later, since their credit score had improved, they were able to get refinanced into a regular lender.

Private lending is about giving solutions.

Real Estate Principal: Mortgages Are Always Paid Out First

Having worked in virtually every area of real estate, I can tell you that "good debt"—in this case money lent out to finance various forms of real estate—will always be a safe bet. Why, you ask? Well, along with the points I mentioned earlier, secured debt is *always paid out first*.

You can always get your money back because it is paid out *before* any equity in that property is calculated. Hence, debt from a lending perspective not only has the potential to yield higher returns but there are avenues in place to *recoup your money* should the deal go south.

The big banks are also well aware that real estate is indeed a safe bet for them. By using the criteria we discussed earlier including income level, levels of bad debt held by borrowers—or the loan-to-value (LTV) ratio—as well as credit scores, the banks lend out money secure in the knowledge that the debt on a mortgage will be paid out before any of the equity or unsecured lenders are paid out.

In other words, they know that they will get their money back. What bank wouldn't be jumping for joy knowing that anything lent can be recouped given the governmental measures put in place *and* they earn interest on their investment. Money speaks and the banks listen!

If a default were to occur for a property that a private lender has contributed resources to, the mortgage is always paid out first, with the exception of city property taxes and sometimes revenue. Just stop to think about what happens when the stock market tanks. Do you make a good return on your investment? Could you perceive this as being a "safe" investment? Remember the control aspect of private lending that we talked about earlier. What control do you have over the volatility of the stock market?

So, if you have not already picked up on the theme of this chapter, *private lending can be a very secure means of investing.*

I am by no way suggesting that playing the stock market is the only other way to invest your money, because there are other avenues open to you. Take mutual funds, for example. Yes, a considerable number of people choose to invest in public stock or mutual funds. When it comes to mutual funds there are key points to keep in mind. You can have something extremely low risk, such as the bond fund, or you can choose an extremely high-risk option such as foreign equities. So, the point I am trying to hammer home here is that there can be a large degree of variance.

Equally important to note is that you will ultimately be paying a substantial fee, called a management expense ratio (MER), which usually amounts to 4 or 5 percent to manage this money every year. So, the return that you make in order to get an 8 percent return must be at least 12 percent, as the management fees swallow up a good portion of the return.

You could explore the prospect of **direct ownership**, but you should not expect to see high returns on your investment. Low to medium returns are more probable and of course you have to deal with the issues that come along with renting out your property, including any tenant issues that may arise.

Joint ventures could be another option, but again you have to work closely with the other parties that agree to invest with you, and this has the potential to open up a can of worms. Working together can certainly cause strain, and I want you to have a relatively painless plan in place to privately lend your money! Stay tuned for the next book in the series that will go in depth on this topic.

Private lending, on the other hand, gives you the control to decide who and how much to lend out and at what rate. If you invest wisely there is far greater potential for higher rates of returns on your real estate investment. I am here to teach you to recognize what is a wise investment in the realm of private lending. I am skilled at giving you the information to ward off any potential pitfalls and to suggest the best ways as a private lender you can invest your money in various real estate ventures at low risk to you.

I know you are ready to play the game. It's a win-win. Not to toot my own horn, but the bulk of the wealth I have acquired for myself, my family, and my clients has been through private lending ventures. I dove into this area without reservation because I know the rewards far outweigh the risks. I also know that you are bound to make a profit from loaning out your money privately for real estate purposes. I also enjoy the control that you inherently have as a private lender.

I love setting the terms of each deal. I also find selecting suitable borrowers is fun, and the interaction you will have with them can also be quite rewarding. You too can start to build your investment portfolio in the ever-changing real estate climate and have fun doing it! Diversify your portfolio and enjoy the ride into the territory of private lending.

As mortgage amounts have increased due to real estate values, being a sole lender has become more difficult. This is one of the reasons I opened our administration company and the mutual fund trust.

Summary

Chapter 1 makes the case for private lending: a lower risk method of investing in real estate that can benefit both lender and borrower. Compared to other methods of investing—such as hedge funds, cryptocurrencies, direct ownership, and stocks—private lending allows the lender greater control of their investment, as they decide their loan structure, terms, interest rate, amount, and who they choose to lend to.

Keywords

Asset: "a resource with economic value that an individual (...) owns or controls with the expectation that it will provide a future benefit."[1]

Bitcoin: a type of cryptocurrency.

Borrower: the individual who receives money from a private lender.

Bridge loan: a short-term loan that allows a borrower to "bridge the gap" between mortgages.

Cryptocurrency: "a digital or virtual currency (...) (often) decentralized networks based on blockchain technology."[2]

Debt: money owed.

Debt-service ratio: "a measurement of (...) available cash flow to pay current debt obligations."[3]

Direct ownership: investing in property directly, rather than investing through lending.[4]

Emerging market: "the markets of developing countries that are rapidly growing and industrializing."[5]

Equity: "the value of a property after you have paid any mortgage or other debts relating to it."[6]

Futures: "derivative financial contracts that obligate the parties to transact an asset at a predetermined future date and price."[7]

Hard Lending/Hard Money Loan: "a loan from a private lender backed by a tangible asset like real estate. These loans usually have shorter terms and higher rates than traditional mortgages."[8]

Hedge fund: "actively managed investment pools whose managers use a wide range of strategies (...) in an effort to beat average investment returns for their clients (...) (which are) considered risky alternative investment choices."[9]

Home equity line of credit (HELOC): loans that are "secured against the equity value of your home."[10]

Initial public offering (IPO): when a "privately owned company lists its shares on a stock exchange, making them available for purchase by the general public."[11]

Joint venture: "a combination of two or more parties that seek the development of a single enterprise or project for profit, sharing the risks associated with its development."[12]

Loan: "a sum of money (...) lent to another party in exchange for future repayment of the value or principal amount."[13]

Loan-to-Value (LTV) ratio: a metric used to measure lending risk, calculated by dividing mortgage amount by appraised property value.[14]

Management expense ratio (MER): a measure of "how much of a fund's assets are used for administrative and other operating expenses (...) determined by dividing a fund's operating expenses by the average dollar value of its assets under management."[15]

Mortgage: "a loan used to purchase or maintain a home, land, or other types of real estate."[16]

Mutual fund: "a company that pools money from many investors and invests the money in securities such as stocks, bonds, and short-term debt."[17]

New construction loan: "a short-term loan that covers only the costs of custom home building."[18]

Options: "financial derivatives that give buyers the right, but not the obligation, to buy or sell an underlying asset at an agreed-upon price and date."[19]

Penny stock: a "stock of a small company that trades for less than $5 per share."[20]

Prospective borrower: an individual who seeks to receive money from a private lender.

Private lending: "when individuals lend their own capital to other investors or professionally managed real estate funds while securing said loan with a mortgage against real estate."[21]

Registered Retirement Savings Plan (RRSP): "a retirement savings and investing vehicle for employees and the self-employed in Canada."[22]

Retirement Income Fund (RIF): "an investment product available to anyone as a conservative means of saving for retirement."[23]

Risk: "the chance that an outcome or investment's actual gains will differ from an expected outcome or return."[24]

Tax-Free Savings Account (TFSA): "a way for individuals who are 18 years of age or older (…) to set money aside tax-free throughout their lifetime."[25]

Security: "an instrument of investment in the form of a document (such as a stock certificate or bond) providing evidence of its ownership."[26]

Self-Directed Registered Retirement Savings Plan (Self-Directed RRSP): "a type of RRSP (…) whose owner determines the asset mix held in the trust."[27]

Stock: "a security that represents the ownership of a fraction of a corporation."[28]

CHAPTER 2: THINKING LIKE A BATTLE-TESTED LENDER

You probably remember how frustrating it was as a child when teachers and parents would tell you that you must learn how to do things step by step. Who has the time? Who has the patience? Can't we just skip a few steps and get to the part that will increase my investment income? I am here to say that like anything, private lending requires you to learn a few steps, but I promise there aren't too many.

Understanding a few principles and some terminology, coupled with a solid foundation, and you will be well on your way. The good news is that the steps it takes to be truly successful as a private lender are easy and straightforward. Don't be intimidated. We will have you lending privately in no time!

Chapter 1 set out to broadly define the area of private lending first and foremost. It then went on to tackle some of the key terminology at play and compared various other investment platforms to the realm of private lending. This has laid your foundation. We are dealing with real estate at the end of the day. What property would sell if it did not have a solid foundation? What private lender could thrive without solid footing in the given area?

Exit Planning

If there is one principle that guides my thinking when it comes to private lending, I would have to say always make sure your borrowers have a real plan for an exit on your loan and have a strategy in place. A simple answer of "We will refinance with a main lender in 12 months" doesn't cut it.

I also believe strongly in setting goals in any endeavour. In the realm of private lending, goal setting is a necessity.

Setting goals is the first step in turning the invisible into the visible.

– Tony Robbins

Let's get back to the real numbers you could be looking at. As a private lender, the interest rates that one could potentially ask for start at about 5 or 6 percent and can go as high as 20 to 25 percent. Yes, those numbers look attractive, but read on about being careful when you are looking at the upper end of the interest rate scale.

Setting Your Interest Rates

Your base rate will be determined by market conditions and the type of lending you do. For example, in Toronto there are a lot of private lenders. This has driven interest rates down. However, in North Bay and Windsor there are very few private lenders. Consequently, the rates are much higher. Since private lending is very real estate focused, you need to be an expert in your marketplace or work with a team that is. First mortgages generally start in the 6 percent range and second mortgages start in the 10 percent range.

The following table gives an idea of how rates generally fall. Each investor and each market will have different factors that will influence the rates and loan-to-values. A word of caution: anything over 80 percent loan-to-value is very risky.

We start off by determining your base interest rate. This is the lowest interest rate you would be willing to accept for an amazing deal. It is important to note, though, that this is just a guide. You need to be flexible. Lenders who are too rigid do not get a lot of mortgages.

The credit classes A, B, and C are a very personal thing. I would avoid trying to use the "score" as a way to classify people. The automated scoring works REALLY well in A lending world, but not so much in the private world. I cover this more in Chapter 7. The scores I put below are just one example and based on an average. Your local market, focus of business will impact these greatly.

Credit Class (with suggested credit score ranges)	Loan-to-Value			
	>65%	65% - 75%	75%-85%	85%+
A (650-plus)	Base Rate - 1%	Base Rate +0%	Base Rate + 1%	Base Rate + 3%
B (550-650)	Base Rate +0%	Base Rate + 1%	Base Rate + 2%	NO
C (ongoing credit problems)	Base Rate + 1%	Base Rate + 2%	Base Rate + 4%	NO

Some Potential Adjustments to Your Base Rate (Example adjustments you may want to use)	
Self-employed	+2%
Currently in power of sale or foreclosure	+4%
Secure employment (i.e., government worker or teacher, etc.)	-1%
Additional security or blanketed property	Reduce rate or increase loan-to-value
Guarantors	Reduce rate or increase loan-to-value

Thinking like a private lender means being flexible. In my brokerage, we had a recent transaction that included a property that had a municipal work order on it. The borrower was working with the city to obtain the property permits to rectify it. However, it looked scary. In reality it wasn't, but the potential pain caused a bit of heartburn. So, we added a guarantor on the file who has a stable job, perfect credit, and a home in the suburbs with equity that more than equalled the loan amount. Thinking like a lender means that you obtain as much security as possible up to the point of losing the deal. Sometimes, asking a few more questions will yield a great result.

You may want to ask yourself why your potential client is willing to pay this steep interest rate. Perhaps the reason is that they had little luck with traditional lending options because of very bad credit or something similar. This is when you have to put on your private lending hat and look for any potential red flags, as we discussed earlier. Do not let greed cloud your judgment. If the market rate for a second mortgage is 14 percent and someone is offering you 20 percent, you need dig a little to find out why. It still may be a good deal, but don't let the shiny coin blind you.

As you approach each deal, I cannot stress enough that you have to keep asking the relevant questions that will help determine whether the deal will work for your investment needs and represent a lucrative option.

Is this potentially a "bad" deal? Can you foresee potential pitfalls? Is the high rate of return worth the risk that may be inherent in this particular deal? Each private lending deal should be scrutinized independently.

The human element is also *very* important. We recently backed away from a deal that would have been very lucrative. The deal checked all the boxes. Good location, nice property, brand new, low loan-to-value ratio, good interest rate, and good fees. However, as I worked with the borrower over a week or so collecting documents, I realized that this person was unstable and very histrionic. I knew that this deal would be a drain on resources and would cause stress and anxiety for my administration team. So, we walked away from the deal. Remember there are *always* people looking for money. Some of the best deals are the deals you didn't do.

You have probably heard the word **opportunity cost** thrown around in financial books or dinner parties full of guests who are "experts" when it comes to finance. I am here to tell you that the notion of opportunity cost or comparing the benefit of a possible outcome against the risk of a negative outcome is at the heart of the way you must think as a private lender.

You have money to lend. You have potential clients to lend out to. Now it is your job to determine who deserves your trust. Ask yourself the hard questions. Look at each deal as a separate entity.

Determine how much you want to lend. Who do you want to lend out to and what interest rate seems reasonable for each private lending deal? You are simply weighing the opportunity cost. Does the likelihood of a positive rate of return on your investment outweigh the small risk that is at play?

Important note: Do not let your guard down just because you may know the borrower. Always follow the steps—do your research, homework, and due diligence. It is your money. Set the parameters.

Remember: This Is a Business

The same rules apply in the realm of private lending as they would in any business. To succeed in any business, you must use the same principles in order to set yourself out from the pack. Applying these principles represents more than half the battle to winning in the private lending industry. Asking yourself a series of important questions sets the groundwork for the deal you eventually negotiate with a potential borrower. Always remember that it is a business.

> Like Airline pilots, create your own checklist or download ours at becomingthebankbook.com

You are not in the position to make friends. You are lending your money in order to make a decent return on your investment. Ask the relevant questions: what is the long-term objective? What are you looking for in a potential borrower? How reliable is your borrower? If your questions are answered to your satisfaction, then you will have the confidence to proceed with structuring your private loan.

Mindset Equals Success

You must think like a lender! Get into the *mindset* of a lender. What do lenders want most? What is the end game? What is the motivation? Just like you can't run before you walk, you can't possibly be a successful lender without *thinking like one.*

The key word to focus on is *mindset.* You are a lender now. Like it or not, you must think like a bank in order to become consistently profitable as a private lender. Focus on the key elements that are at play and look at them from the lending perspective.

Mental preparedness is so important when you are contemplating private lending. Know what you want from the outset. Seek out only the borrowers that fit your overall picture of what you want to achieve. Make sure to put your private lending hat securely on and let it guide your decisions as a private lender. The sky's the limit when you truly think like a private lender!

Think Like a Bank

Yes, it is no secret that the big banks have perfected the mindset of the lender and have used all strategies to their advantage. What do the banks want? Same thing as you—the greatest maximum return on the smallest amount of leveraged money. The banks charge **fees**. You also definitely want to charge as many fees as possible. When it comes to **money**, the banks limit what they lend out. You should also lend out as little as possible. As far as **interest rates**, well, the banks have cornered this market! The higher the better! Put yourself first and set out the parameters for your borrowers. The banks use this way of thinking every day. Now it is your turn!

Fees: You definitely want to charge as many fees as possible.

Money: Lend out as little as possible.

Interest rates: The higher the better!

What do the banks want? Exactly what you want. Put as little money in at the lowest risk and achieve the highest rate of return.

The dream scenario would look like this. A client approaches you with 50 percent down on a property (less money is needed to lend out because they already have half of what is needed). The client is willing to pay the fees that you deem necessary for the deal. You are able to secure a 10 percent interest on the money that you lend out (have you seen the interest credit cards charge?). Think like a bank and put that private lending hat securely on your head.

Of course, not every deal will look like this. However, it occurs often enough. I am simply illustrating the mindset you must have as well as the goals you must keep in mind to profit best as a private lender. You must train yourself to not only ask the questions necessary to enter into a lucrative private deal, but to also focus on the mentality you must have to be a successful private lender.

Do you know about the rate fee offset formula?
Rates or fees equal the same return over 12 months. A 5 percent rate and a 3 percent fee equals 8 percent a year. Some deals work with lower rate and higher fee or vice versa. Also, most fees are deducted from the advance so it is earned immediately.

So, if you think the loan will be paid off before the end of the term, a higher fee and lower rate will earn you a higher return.

I often look at what motivational techniques or mentalities are necessary for high performance athletes to succeed. Yes, winning is the end goal. The question is, how do you get from point A (training) to point B (winning)? In my opinion, like everything in life, it boils down to 90 percent mental and 10 percent skill. Athletes are very focused and need to be in the right mindset to focus on winning. They are always perfecting their skillset but rely on laser focus to be successful.

You might be questioning me at this point because I just finished telling you that there are necessary skills required to succeed as a private lender, and building the foundation is one of them. I stand by this. However, if you do not focus on the mindset then the skills will only take you so far. Bottom line to take away: think like a private lender while always honing your skills.

How you succeed in business works the same as how you succeed in private lending. Borrowers are not your friends! You are making an informed investment and you need to see your money back with interest earned. Select borrowers with this in mind, not whether they like you or vice versa. As the age-old saying goes, "You may want to keep your friends close, but in private lending definitely keep your borrowers closer!"

Summary

Chapter 2 lays out the rules of private lending, advising you to "think like a bank": charge as many fees as possible, lend as little money as possible, and opt for the highest possible interest rates.

Keywords

Exit planning: "the complete strategy for exiting a privately held company"[29] or private lending contract.

Fee: "a fixed price charged for a specific service."[30]

Human element: a factor relating to the individual and personal aspects of individuals (lender and borrower) making a deal, e.g., trustworthiness.

Interest rate: "the amount charged on top of the principal by a lender to a borrower for the use of assets."[31]

Opportunity cost: "the forgone benefit that would have been derived from an option not chosen."[32]

Rate fee offset formula: negotiating and setting rates and fees in a deal in order to achieve the desired return.

CHAPTER 3: HITTING THE BULLSEYE WITH LOAN-TO-VALUE AND INTEREST RATES

Depending on the interest rate you have determined, the level of risk also comes into play. In a **lower loan-to-value** deal, there is lower risk associated, but with lower rates as a result. In a **higher loan-to-value** deal there is more risk attached, but with the potential of charging much higher interest rates. Ask yourself, are you willing to lend out money at a very high interest rate such as a second mortgage, or would you rather stick with lending opportunities that are inherently less "risky" but will yield smaller returns on your investment?

For example, if you are comfortable lending out second or even third mortgages, for which you can charge double-digit interest rates, the potential to yield very high returns is there. This is an example of a **higher loan-to-value** deal. Keep in mind, however, that the risk is higher than lending out money toward a first mortgage at a lower interest rate.

It is important to remember that risk is a relative term. In general, mortgages, when done correctly, are on the lower end of the risk spectrum, as covered earlier. I like to use the example of cars, since I am a car guy. Driving down the road at 50 miles per hour in a car is normally very safe and very low risk. You have all the safety of roll cages, seat belts, air bags, and more. If you got into an accident, chances are you would be fine. However, drive down the same road on a bicycle at 50 miles per hour and get into an accident, the story may not be so rosy. Mortgages are the same. Both activities have risks, but you need to put them in relative terms. After reading this book, you will be driving down the road in a brand-new Volvo, wearing a helmet.

What Loan-to-Value Should You Aim For?

One of the most important criteria that mortgage professionals have always paid considerable attention to when structuring mortgage deals with their clients is looking at the amount the borrower is asking to borrow against the value and how much they can put down toward the mortgage. In other words, what are they willing and able to put down at the outset and how much will they be borrowing? It is not only mortgage professionals that are making this distinction. You can rest assured the banks have it down to a very well-oiled formula!

Loan-to-Value (LTV) = Mortgage Amount/Value

Typically, banks and mortgage professionals have always looked at **75 to 80 percent loan-to-value** as being a very comfortable margin when loaning money for mortgages. You would be wise to follow the banks and aim for the same loan-to-value on your mortgage deals that you structure. Of course, as I have pointed out more than once throughout these early chapters, as a private lender you ultimately have the control to decide what loan-to-value you are comfortable with when you structure your mortgage loans. You can lend to 100 percent or even higher if you wish.

Example

If a potential borrower approaches you with the request for financing at the widely accepted 80 percent loan-to-value, you will be looking at a 20 percent down payment for this loan.

- The value is $200,000
- The down payment is $40,000
- The loan request should be $160,000
- This represents 80 percent financing (80 percent loan-to-value)

In general, I would certainly feel comfortable loaning out a mortgage like the one above. The banks would also look at this as a low-risk loan-to-value loan. Another reason an 80 percent loan-to-value is the gold standard in the mortgage industry relates to insurance. If a borrower is able to put down 20 percent toward financing a mortgage, then there is no need to apply for mortgage insurance.

The banks will not require the government to insure this mortgage deal. Mortgage insurance is an added expense for the borrower and is rolled into the overall monthly payments for the borrower. Obviously, this increases the borrower's monthly overall mortgage payments. The point to be made here for our purposes is that, if the banks and large financial institutions consider a deal under the 80 percent loan-to-value, it is considered risky enough to require insurance coverage. Keep in mind that in the realm of private lending, default insurance is not applicable, which is why you can set your interest rates so high on potentially riskier loan-to-value mortgage loans that you may consider negotiating.

A Few More Things to Keep in Mind When Addressing Loan-to-Value

It is advisable to try to mirror the banks in terms of the loan-to-value mortgage you negotiate with your borrower. It would be beneficial for you to be familiar with what type of credit you should be looking for in your borrowers in order to feel comfortable in the type of loan you negotiate with them. After reading Chapter 7 on credit, the type of borrower will become more apparent to you. Here is a quick reference guide for you to chew on in the meantime:

When classifying potential borrowers based on their comprehensive credit history and track record in terms of paying back creditors, mortgage professionals generally classify borrowers in three credit categories. (Other criteria come into play, such as available down payment, employment history, and other assets the borrowers may have.) These categories include:

1. **A Clients**: They will have an overall credit score of 650-plus and are considered the lowest risk clients to lend to.

2. **B Clients:** These clients have an overall credit score of 500-650 and are considered for some loans and are viewed as medium risk clients to lend to.

3. **C Clients:** These clients may have ongoing credit problems and other black marks that may affect securing traditional loans and are considered as such to be higher risk borrowers.

Something else to note: a person's credit history is very much the story of their financial life. You will learn to read a credit report and see what kind of people they are. For example, you will be able to see if they had a major life event, such as a bankruptcy, or default on a previous loan, or if they overspend.

Remember: a credit score is only *part* of a person's credit story. You need to understand the entire report.

The classification of borrowers that mortgage professionals make is important to know when it comes time for you to determine the overall loan-to-value you are comfortable with when structuring your mortgage contract. As a general rule of thumb, you can base your loan-to-value mortgages on the following guidelines:

1. **More than 85 percent loan-to-value:** You will need to secure an A credit borrower. This high loan-to-value loan is **not considered secure** and as a result you will need to secure other collateral beyond the property in question to secure your funds, such as a motorcycle, car, or another property. In this case you can add an **interest rate premium** and charge more than you would normally for another mortgage loan.

2. **75 to 80 percent loan-to-value**: With this loan-to-value loan, you will be able to access A, B, and C borrowers. It is considered somewhat secure and may need extra collateral. You can consider charging a slight interest premium.

3. **65 to 75 percent loan-to-value**: Again, with this loan you can access all levels of credit borrowers. It is generally considered a

secure loan and will not need extra collateral or a need to charge an interest premium.

4. **Less Than 65 percent loan-to-value:** This is an example of a low loan-to-value loan and as a result it is very secure. The borrower is borrowing less against the value of the property, as such there will be no need for extra collateral or interest rate premiums.

Additional Circumstances to Consider Charging Interest Rate Premiums

As you can see, there are some high loan-to-value loans that you may be negotiating, namely high loan-to-value loans over 85 percent, where you will most certainly be advised to charge extra interest rate premiums. This stems from the risk to reward ratio. The lower the loan-to-value, the lower the risk. The higher the loan-to-value, the potential for higher risk.

To compensate for the greater risk inherent in the high loan-to-value deals, as a private lender it is within your capacity to charge additional interest on your loan (and interest rate premiums).

This is why unsecured loans such as personal loans, note loans, and other similar loans normally have rates well above 30 percent. Note loans and personal loans have *no* security. Do not be fooled unless specific security is given.

This relates, again, to the **risk to reward** rule I keep alluding to. If you're willing to take on a loan with up to 100 percent financing, or—heaven forbid—unsecured note loans, then you will be risking more, but the potential for a greater profit is inherent, too. You will be able to make more from higher interest gained on the loan and this can offset the risk often associated with such high loan-to-value loans.

Two Examples Where Interest Rate Premiums Make Sense

1. **Self-Employed or Non-Conventional Income**

    If you are approached by a borrower who may have his or her own business or makes their income from sources that are not easily calculated, then you have a good motivation for charging an interest rate premium. Obviously, a salary and predictable income is easier to calculate the numbers as a private lender.

As such, if you accept a borrower who is self-employed, then you can reasonably charge an extra interest rate premium. In this instance you could comfortably attach a **1 to 2 percent interest premium** on top of the interest rate decided upon for this loan. This opens the door for substantial additional profit from this loan. The additional interest on the loan will help to offset any additional risk associated with it.

2. A Property Under Power of Sale

If you eventually consider providing funds toward a mortgage loan on a property that is already under power of sale due to borrower default, then you will have to be willing to ask all the right questions and thoroughly do your research on the history of the property and credit history of the borrower. This example obviously represents a higher risk loan by the sheer nature that there has been an ongoing issue in terms of the existing mortgage on the property.

However, the flip side when considering such a loan is that you will have the green light to add extra interest charge premiums on the loan. In this case you can reasonably ask for a **4 percent interest rate premium or more** in addition to the agreed-upon interest rate.

Having said this, let's circle back to the fundamentals and distinctive advantages of setting yourself up as a private lender. You have the control and flexibility to determine for yourself what type of mortgage loan you will be setting up with your borrower. So, if you feel comfortable with a 90 to 95 percent or even 100 percent loan-to-value, then you can arrange this with your borrower. However, I would advise you to not loan out this type of high loan-to-value mortgage for a long period of time or term. Try to recoup your money in the short term with high loan-to-value mortgages.

I have had quite a few clients who are in their golden years who are very successful private lenders. They choose to lend out money toward low to moderate risk deals such as the first mortgage on a property. Again, this is a good example of a **lower loan-to-value** deal. The interest rates attached to deals such as this usually falls within the 5 to 6 percent interest rate territory.

> Using the rule of 72, with an interest rate of 6 percent your money would double in approximately 12 years. More about the rule of 72 later.

On the other hand, there are plenty of private investors who are looking for high returns on their investments and lucrative deals. As such, they are charging interest rates as high as 20 percent on third mortgages. The potential for default may come into play, but remember what we talked about earlier, in a real estate venture the **mortgage is always paid out first**.

Take note that if you are interested in the higher risk deals it is important to have clearly established procedures in place in case there is a default. To protect yourself, make sure that you keep track of all payments and do not allow for a missed payment.

In a **higher loan-to-value file,** it is essential that you run a very tight ship in order to be successful and have the necessary protection in place to recoup your money if it becomes necessary. I will talk further about this in Chapter 5 when we discuss the very important element of default management and protecting your assets.

Essentially, in private lending it comes down to determining your comfort level, which is a skill that is key to success in the realm of private lending. Once your comfort level is established, then it is much easier to meet your objectives and set your long-term investment goals.

Summary

Chapter 3 takes a closer look at loan-to-value (LTV). LTV is calculated by using the formula, LTV Mortgage amount/Value. Low LTV means there is less associated risk, but also lower interest rates. High LTV means there is more risk attached, but the potential to charge high interest rates. To assess risks, private lenders mirror the banks by categorizing prospective buyers according to their credit score.

Keywords

Compound interest: "the interest on a loan or deposit calculated based on both the initial principal and the accumulated interest from previous periods."[33]

Credit score: "three-digit number that comes from the information in your credit report (showing) how well you manage credit and how risky it would be for a lender to lend you money."[34]

Interest rate premiums: additional interest designed to mitigate risk for the lender. **Risk/Reward Ratio:** "the prospective reward an investor can earn for every dollar they risk on an investment."[35]

CHAPTER 4: THE FIVE Cs OF PRIVATE LENDING—FIVE STEPS TO LENDING SUCCESS

I am taking you on a journey through the exciting and often uncharted territory of private lending. Like any journey, sometimes we have to re-trace our steps in order to move forward. Having said this, let's go back to the building blocks of private lending. Your kids probably spend hours putting together Lego pieces and then tackle puzzles. To really get to the heart of this business, you should too. Without the thorough knowledge of this area of investing, it becomes difficult to ultimately put together lucrative deals.

I know that you probably don't want another lesson on the fundamentals of private lending, but I can assure you that if you incorporate what I am saying in this chapter you will have information that will serve you very well in your new career as a private lender.

I am now going to introduce you to the **five Cs of lending**. Any banker worth his or her salt has been trained on the five Cs. It is a great way weed out people that don't really know the business. Each lender will rank the Cs in an order that is most important to them. When I lend, I use the ranking below. They are all very important, but the one everyone agrees on is number one. I find that number five, character, won't help get someone approved but it will definitely make me decline someone.

One year, I was reviewing a file over the holidays. The properties—there were two of them—where A+. The loan-to-value was 65 percent in Toronto. However, as I was dealing with the borrower over the holidays, I began to see a personality pattern I did not like. I knew this person would be high maintenance and a drain on my staff resources. We would most likely have come out of the deal okay, but the extra effort would not have been worth it. You will not be able to structure a private mortgage loan that you are comfortable with until you take each of the five Cs under consideration.

1. Collateral: Can I Sell This House?

This is what you are pinning your investment hopes against in many instances. It's your safety net, so to speak. This is why it is critical to know your collateral inside out. Of course, when we are referring to collateral, we are referring to the house that you are securing your loan against. It is so important that you research this property thoroughly. Know the specifics of the house, and equally important, get to know the neighbourhood thoroughly.

What are comparable properties or similar houses selling for in the area? Is this area desirable? How much have properties been appreciating or depreciating in the neighbourhood? What is happening to the overall economy in the region? This is even more important in the post-COVID-19 era.

If you are uncomfortable just relying on this property to secure your loan, you do have the option of structuring what is referred to in the mortgage industry as a **blanket mortgage**. In this type of mortgage loan, you can require your borrower to include another property as collateral to secure the loan. This represents the loan being registered to the principal property and an additional property. This may give you a greater sense of ease or control over the direction of your loan. It also provides you with the legal right to go after both properties to recoup your money.

Obtain the appraisal on the property and review it thoroughly. This is a document that will give you invaluable information about the value of the property and its relative value. At the same time, you should be very familiar with the real estate market and how it pertains to the property. **Obtain the Multiple Listing Service (MLS)** on the property and review it thoroughly as well. The appraisal is so important I have dedicated Chapter 12 to it.

Once you have become familiar with what is articulated in the appraisal, then I would now suggest that you obtain a second opinion on the appraisal. Cover your bases and refer to more than one expert on the property in question. Last, it is imperative to get a **letter of direction** pertaining to the property *directly* from the appraisers. This is covered in greater detail in Chapter 12, but in effect it is a letter authorizing who can use the appraisal.

You cannot be too thorough when doing your due diligence with the property that serves as collateral for your mortgage loan. Use every means to research your property and be familiar with all aspects pertaining to it is in your best interest. It will serve you well when you are putting together your mortgage deals as a private lender.

2. Credit: Have They Reliably Paid?

This is fitting, as I devote Chapter 7 to the fundamental importance of credit when negotiating a private mortgage loan. I cannot stress enough the importance that credit scores and credit history play in the overall factoring of choosing your potential borrower. You need to be very familiar with the potential borrower's overall credit picture. Look for patterns in their ability and consistency in paying bills and creditors. Look out for any potential red flags.

Just for fun, I recommend pulling your own credit report from one of the main credit reporting agencies: Equifax, TransUnion, or Experian. It is free to pull your credit report. It's useful to know your overall credit standing and beacon credit score. It's also useful to be extremely familiar with the criteria the credit agencies are using to determine an individual's credit worthiness. You will be scrutinizing many credit reports moving forward, and knowledge is power.

Don't forget to allow for credit dips due to unforeseen life events. These borrowers most likely have blemished credit. That is why they are talking to you and not a bank.

Enough said—you get it!

3. Capacity: Can They Pay?

It is imperative to look at all the variables that come into play that demonstrate an ability for your borrower to comfortably pay back money that is lent to them. Focus on any income streams ranging from their salary to secondary income like freelance work. Also look at other means your borrower has to produce income, including rental properties or other investments producing solid returns.

You want to make sure that your borrower has the required financial resources to pay you back reliably and to make their monthly payments plus interest accruing on the loan. Any additional sources of income beyond the principal salary should be scrutinized and taken into account to paint a complete financial picture of your potential borrower.

Do they have the means to carry through reliably with payments moving forward? Make sure that they are in the financial position to take on a second or even third mortgage including their daily and monthly expenditures and/or other loan payment requirements. Again, think like a bank. Make sure you look at all potential revenue streams open to your borrower and their fiscal responsibility.

4. Capital: What Resources Do They Have?

This is fairly self-explanatory and relates directly to their overall capacity to pay. What other sources of cash or resources are available to your borrowers? How many assets do they own? What investments have they secured? Anything generating money or things they could sell or cash in would fall into this category and affects their overall capacity to pay you back. Capital provides security and leverage in which to lend out further money. Look at capital as the financial assets while capacity is their overall ability to pay.

5. Character: What Impression Do They Give You?

I cannot stress this point enough. The lending business is first and foremost a people business. You are dealing with people on a one-on-one basis, and you are developing a working relationship with them. A big part of formulating any relationship, business or otherwise, is to get a feeling of what makes your borrower or client tick. Learning about his or her personality and painting a picture of them based on their past experiences and reactions to life events.

By knowing your client's overall character, you can base your decision on whether you feel they would be a reliable individual to lend money to. Are they respectful, honest, consistent, and loyal? Traits such as these would help you assess whether you want to continue in a working relationship with him/her and provide you with the confidence to lend money out to them.

Having said this, it is entirely possible to lend out your money to borrowers that you have not met or have had limited contact with. If this is the case then you will be basing your borrowing criteria on their credit worthiness, ability to pay you, and overall financial picture, including substantial assets.

When you are putting your private lender cap on, you are making many decisions and asking yourself many questions. All of your decisions should be geared to structuring the best possible mortgage loan and finding the best possible borrowers to lend your money to. Paint a picture of your borrower by pulling together all relevant bits of financial information and personality traits and piecing together a mortgage loan like a jigsaw puzzle. Account for every important piece of the puzzle and making sure all pieces fit perfectly to create a seamless and lucrative mortgage deal.

Think of the five Cs as the hanger on which to hang the dress or the outline in which to formulate your overall business plan. This relates to the foundation that we are continuously building as we progress into the technical aspects of the field of private lending. When structuring your deal, you will be using the five Cs to form the skeleton of your deal. This does not mean that you will not need to be flexible when negotiating each loan, depending on your borrowers' circumstances or particular issues pertaining to each specific loan you hammer out.

Summary

Chapter 4 teaches the five Cs of private lending: collateral (whether the house will be easy to sell), credit (whether the borrower has reliably paid), capacity (whether the borrower is able to pay), capital (what resources the borrower has), and character (what impression the borrower gives).

Keywords

Appraisal: "a valuation of a property (...) by the estimate of an authorized person."[36]

Blanket mortgage: "a single mortgage that covers two or more pieces of real estate."[37]

Capacity: "the borrower's ability to repay a loan by comparing income against recurring debts."[38]

Capital: "accumulated assets (as money) invested or available for investment."[39]

Collateral: "property (such as securities) pledged by a borrower to protect the interests of the lender."[40]

Multiple Listing Service (MLS): "a database established by cooperating real estate brokers to provide data about properties for sale."[41]

CHAPTER 5: JUST HOW ARE YOU GOING TO FIND THESE BORROWERS?

If the five Cs of private lending are of importance (which they are!), then we cannot finish this conversation without talking about just how you go about finding the best borrowers. This is obviously one of the key ingredients that go into the mix when you are formulating your overall business plan moving forward. Without borrowers there is no deal.

Without good borrowers, you are not going to be able to formulate the deals with the highest potential returns and develop a satisfying working relationship with your future clients. The key to your success is being able to find and pinpoint potential borrowers with the best financial capabilities, strong assets and credit history and beacon scores.

The question then becomes: just how are you, as a private lender, going to go about finding these quality borrowers and where? The answer lies in a number of reliable sources and avenues.

A word of caution before we continue with our conversation. It is advisable to *not* look for borrowers through advertising channels like online classifieds or newspapers. In order to advertise, you will need a licence. The banks and licensed mortgage brokers are able to use these resources because they have the licence that enables them to do so. **However, there is one exception to this rule.**

If you advertise in a specific way, you will be able to advertise through some of these advertising channels. It is imperative that you, as a lender, state in the ad that you specifically have your **own funds** that you can **lend directly to a borrower**. If it is not worded this way, it may be deemed an illegal form of advertising. It is illegal because you would require a **mortgage licence** to loan funds any other way.

On a further note, do not use in your advertising terminology the word "guarantee," as this may have legal ramifications. Running your ad by a lawyer would be beneficial to ensure that you are not using jargon that may misrepresent yourself and be deemed against the law for non-licensed lenders.

Preferred Ways to Find the Best Borrowers

Investment Clubs and Professional Organizations

I would suggest focusing your attention toward professionals to supply you with a pool of desirable potential borrowers. In their business dealings as well as among their circle of clients and acquaintances, professionals such as accountants, lawyers, realtors, and mortgage brokers will be able to suggest potential reliable borrowers to you.

Professions such as medicine, law, and accounting have professional bodies and associations where you can find potential borrowers with the kind of criteria that you are looking for as private lenders. The criteria of the five Cs that you are looking to assess a potential client will likely be favourable among individuals within these professions and associations.

You can take it a step further and contact various **investment groups**. An investment group is a group made up of investors that meet on a regular basis to discuss topics pertaining to investing. They are also on the lookout for good investment opportunities and could very well be willing to borrow money from you to finance new properties or resale properties or even rental properties.

Warning! Private notes are unsecured. Do not do them.

If you were to research where some of these groups are and contact their website or directly you are bound to find good borrowers. Start networking now and make some valuable contacts who could turn out to be borrowers that you can negotiate mortgage loans with down the road.

With proper research you will find that there are investment groups in most cities across the country or large urban areas. A note of caution at investment groups. Many of these borrowers will try and sell you a deal that they believe is a good one but often times is not. Always have a neutral third-party review your files when possible. A second set of eyes will keep you out of trouble.

Real Estate and Mortgage Professionals

Do not overlook real estate and mortgage professionals to help you in your search for potential borrowers. With a mortgage professional, he or she has a finger on the pulse of who is in need. An added advantage is that these borrowers have essentially already been screened by professionals who are more than familiar with what is required to be a reliable borrower.

This does not mean that you will not judge each borrower based on your criteria as well. It does, however, ensure that this pool of potential borrowers have been recommended, which represents a solid lead to base your final decision on.

The professionals that you turn to will also represent a steady flow of potential new clients. This in itself is invaluable. You will most likely be screening your own borrowers, however, to have a stream of borrowers to choose from is highly beneficial. This provides the opportunity for money to be lent out continuously to a group of qualified borrowers.

You ideally want to keep your money moving without any interruptions in the flow of capital. As time goes by and you establish yourself as a desirable investor, your professional contacts will reserve their best clients to work with you, which is also a highly desirable position to be in as a private lender.

Don't Forget to Use Your Personal Network of Family and Friends

I am sure that you have turned to your friends and family for different reasons, including networking when looking for a job or finding a pet or maybe just to hit them up for some nice food! Well, when it comes to looking for the right kind of borrowers, family and friends may be a reliable source. You just never know who they may have run into or know through an acquaintance. This opens up a wider pool of potential borrowers at your fingertips. Family first! However, do not lend out directly to family and friends.

With a steady supply of qualified borrowers in addition to a list of professional contacts in which to refer to, you are well on your way to building the client portfolio in which to succeed in the realm of private lending. It is critical that you keep your money lent out without interruptions. This fluidity of your capital is essential when working as a private lender. This will give you a constant stream of business, which is ultimately the aim when you are building your private lending career.

At the end of the day, becoming a lender is really all about developing strong working relationships with your borrowers. You are lending your money out to people. An understanding of the attributes that are most favourable in a borrower is important.

Summary

Chapter 5 discusses ways in which a private lender can find quality borrowers, including: investment groups and professional organizations, real estate and mortgage professionals, and networks of family and friends.

Keywords

Investment group: a group made up of investors that meet on a regular or semi-regular basis to discuss topics pertaining to investing.

CHAPTER 6: THE MORTGAGE MENU

Your borrowers are lined up and you have a steady stream of contacts and potential clients. Now what type of mortgage are you going to lend out? What type of loan are you looking to negotiate? It really boils down to **four types of mortgages**. You will be deciding between different categories of mortgages and basing your decisions on what type of return you would like to earn or what level of risk you are willing to take. The terms first, second, third, etc., relate the legal ranking of secured debt on a property. Here are the general priority rankings on a property:

- Priority A: government of Canada in some circumstances
- Priority B: municipal taxes
- Priority C: condo fees and arrears
- 1st mortgages
- 2nd mortgages
- 3rd mortgages, and so on

The rank stems from the time it is legally registered. Let's say that Scotia Bank gives a mortgage on March 1st, and you give a mortgage on

March 10th. Scotia would have the first mortgage and you would have a second mortgage.

Now let's pretend Scotia's lawyers messed up and didn't register their mortgage until March 15th. You would technically have a first mortgage.

First Mortgage

Typical rates range from 6 to 10 percent.

This is arguably the type of mortgage loan that carries with it little to virtually no risk. If you are first starting out in the private lending field, you may feel more comfortable negotiating this type of first mortgage loan. This is the type of loan that the banks lend out most frequently with varying amortization lengths. As a private lender it is advisable that you limit your loan to three years and include a clause that will allow for a provision of renewal.

An advantage to this type of mortgage loan is that it provides quite a bit of flexibility in terms you may or may not include in your contract. There are some clauses of course that you absolutely should not overlook, such as the power to sale clause.

In addition, the interest rate that you can set on this type of mortgage loan traditionally falls somewhere between 6 and 10 percent. Getting your feet wet in the private lending field may be less of an adjustment with this type of loan. The first mortgage is the mortgage of choice for the big banks as they have years of experience that tells them that this is the lowest risk loan that they can issue. They have little to invest at a decent interest rate and are virtually assured to get their money back. You are a private lender and should be taking all your cues from the banks. Now you can reap the rewards. Novel but true!

Second Mortgage

Typical Rates range from 8 to 15 percent.

If you are very comfortable with a particular borrower who may have come to you upon recommendation from a reliable contact, lending out a second mortgage on an existing property may fit the bill. If the five Cs have been satisfied—**collateral** is firmly in place, **credit** is all stable, the borrower has the overall financial **capacity** to pay back the loan, demonstrated **capital** and a suitable **character**—then providing money for a second mortgage is a sound route to take.

Yes, second mortgages may be inherently more risk based than traditional first-time mortgages but still relatively low risk when compared to other traditional forms of investing. The flip side to remember, however, is that you can easily set interest rates on your loans at somewhere between 10 and 22 percent! Potential for high rates of return is always present in these types of mortgage loans.

A note of caution: When contemplating loaning out second mortgages, it is best to ensure that, if needed, you can cover the costs of a first payment for any hiccups that may occur. As second lender you have the right to cover any default of the first mortgage (make the monthly payments) and take control of the default process. You, in essence, make that mortgage payment while you are selling the home. Second mortgages have the advantage of being quite profitable for the private lender and are still considered relatively low risk in terms of the overall likelihood of seeing all the money paid in full at the end of the term of the loan.

Third Mortgage

Typical rates start at 15 percent.

Once you are considering negotiating the terms of a mortgage loan that is a third mortgage on a property you are entering an area of lending that carries with it a much higher risk. The client has already taken out a mortgage on a property and then a second mortgage. By the time you are looking at a third mortgage the terms are quite different. In this case you may want to revisit the idea of a blanket mortgage loan so you're securing your loan against more than the principal property.

Typically, the interest rates you can set on your loan exceed 20 percent, but the money must be loaned out for a very short term to ensure you recoup your capital. These short-term mortgage loans have a high rate of return, but you must view them as "walk away" loans. Protect yourself in the way you structure these loans and keep the mortgage term short and sweet to recoup your money plus a healthy interest return on your investment.

Bridge Loans

Rates vary here, but a setup fee ranges from 1 to 5 percent of the loan amount.

The fourth type of mortgage loan is slightly different from the other three. It is not a loan for long term, but a loan that will take the borrower through a specific period of time, usually quite limited, until funds become available.

Typically, these loans are very short term. Maybe a couple of months or more to cover a gap in financing between mortgages or between properties being sold.

A bridge loan literally creates a bridge for financing that would not otherwise exist to provide for a crossing between mortgages. Perhaps a client may have put in an offer on a new property and before their current house closes, they will need temporary financing to carry through until both properties close.

Rates on these types of loans stand at around 10 percent plus any additional fees that may incur. Not every lender will provide a bridge loan to their clients. If you do consider this type of loan as an alternative, you should expect low to medium risk from this type of loan and a very short term before you should expect to recoup your money.

Syndicated Mortgages: Another Mortgage Worth Exploring

Exploring different types of mortgages is at the heart of private lending. Deciding on what type of mortgage you will be venturing into is the first step in developing your lending portfolio. One type of mortgage that we have yet to discuss is syndicated mortgage. This mortgage is similar to the other mortgages that we discussed earlier. Syndicated lending differs in that instead of having only one person, bank, or institution funding the mortgage you have several people funding the mortgage, or several institutions and clients.

Let's take the example of a $100,000 mortgage. In this scenario, you may have five investors each with $20,000 to invest. These five investors will share equally one-fifth of the mortgage loan. They could invest the funds through any source available to them including cash, RRSPs, or TFSAs. You might think that this is really complicated and wonder what would motivate you to enter into this type of lender relationship.

I can tell you that syndicated lending can be really advantageous and can help you in many different ways. First of all, it helps to diversify money over multiple transactions. In other words, if you only had $100,000 to invest in mortgages, by entering into a syndicated mortgage at $20,000 each, the chances of you losing all the $100,000 is very small. The chance of all five deals going south is greatly reduced. You basically have averaged out your risk. Remember how the banks think: lend out as little as possible at minimal risk and at rates that are to your advantage!

Second, you can argue that a syndicated mortgage is advantageous in that it allows you to play far above your weight class. You now have access to much larger deals that you could normally not have the leverage to be a part of. Typically, the majority of these larger deals are first mortgages. By nature, they require a lot more capital that a small investor will likely not have access to.

So, by being part of a mortgage syndicate represents a great opportunity to take a piece of a typical first mortgage pie and still be at a low risk to you! You can have your pie and eat it too! It's very common in my practice to do first mortgages on residential properties and residential land especially in major urban centres. These mortgages are usually hundreds of thousands of dollars. It's not that common for one individual to want to put $500,000 on one investment. It is much easier to bring five $100,000 investors, which is an easier pill to swallow for investors that are sharing one-fifth of the return. These first mortgages typically have interest rates between 6 and 8 percent interest. As discussed earlier, first-time mortgages tend to be relatively low loan-to-value—50 to 70 percent—when you are dealing with solid properties generally located in major urban centres.

The likelihood of these properties losing 30 or 40 percent of their value, while it's theoretically possible, is very unlikely. I would call this a safe bet in an industry that will always carry an element of risk to it. This mortgage arrangement creates a really nice safety net for people and their investments. I typically like to do these deals for my senior clients or clients that may be looking for a good income stream and security and low-risk portfolio. These potential investors are willing to take a little less return for a stable cash flow and principal preservation.

The administrator and syndication partner is key here. Ensure you have your lawyer review any syndication and administration documents. **Check to make sure your administrator is licensed in the province you are dealing in.**

> A client approached our brokerage to refinance their home and combine the first and private second mortgage together. We had this all arranged with a new bank. One of the conditions was a statement from the current private lender. It turns out the client was in default and missed over six months of payments. The client was adamant that she was not and sent proof that she was e-transferring the payment every month.
>
> It turns out the lender was working with an unlicensed and unregulated Mortgage Administrator that collected the payments but never gave them to the lender.

The Flipside of Syndicated Mortgages— Deals Gone Sour

Syndicated mortgages are nothing new. If you think about it, dating back for as long as we can remember, people have been lending money in groups. It was very common in ancient Babylon for five or six people with five or six pieces of gold to lend out money to you. Fast forward to our modern context and, unfortunately, we've had examples of some pretty nefarious players using syndicated mortgages to do things that they shouldn't be doing!

Not long ago, a few nefarious players in Ontario were using syndicated mortgage rules to put clients into projects that they really didn't understand. They were also not properly pricing the risk for those investments.

By this point in the book, you should already have realized that one of the benefits of mortgage lending is that it's risk-based pricing. What that means is that the higher the risk of a mortgage the higher the interest rate you should be charging. Now this is not a perfect market as I see some people overcharging low-risk files.

I just recently came across a client that was being charged exorbitant interest rates and fees by another broker. They did a $30,000 second mortgage at 23 percent interest rate plus fees. This poor family paid $7,000 in broker fees and the loan-to-value was less than 35 percent. In this case, the couple both had a good job and their credit was decent. The effective rate of these mortgages was 46 percent interest.

This is nothing short of highway robbery! The clients were definitely not being charged based on their risk profile. They were taken advantage of, but they didn't have a good knowledgebase, so they believed what they were told. Luckily, when it came up for renewal, a lawyer got involved as an independent legal advice requirement and they were referred over to me.

We have now put these clients into a regular first mortgage with a large conventional lender and their interest rate is a bit below 3 percent. As an ethical investor it is important to charge a fair rate of return. There is almost an infinite number of deals out there. You do not need to rob people!

Circling back to risk-based pricing, bringing in inexperienced investors or residential investors—that really represented average workers with families—to invest in large construction projects of multi-million-dollar condos was another form of misinformation. These average investors were swallowed up in huge multi-million-dollar deals investing only a few hundred thousand dollars.

That in itself is not a bad thing, and it's been happening for decades all across Canada and all across North America. It is very typical for developers and builders to go and obtain syndicated mortgages or equity investors to build their condo towers. We have been putting deals like this together, like I just mentioned, for decades. The difference here was that they're bringing in investors that didn't understand what they were actually lending on.

More recently, proper disclosures, which should have been there from the start, are getting better and are becoming the norm in lending. This type of thing is not rocket science and would have saved a lot of heartache and confusion if lenders had been required to be transparent long ago. **Simply put: if you do not understand the deal then do not invest or lend.**

I have to add that the interest rate charged and the interest rate that these investors received was not consummate to the risk. When you're partially investing in equity on a development project, you're typically talking a 20 to 25 percent return. You can bet that somewhere along the way there is a high probability that you will end up in some kind of issue with a project of this magnitude.

Development and land deals will often get delayed, and there will be restructuring as a result. It is quite common for development projects to go through a period of instability before it's built. Knowing all these variables would have served as warning signs to average investors.

I was recently working with one developer who had a very sophisticated process, is very well known, and had pre-sold a bunch of condos in Southern Ontario. Unfortunately, the construction cost of this project escalated extremely quickly, far more than the builder had allocated for in his budget. This occurred despite him being highly experienced and a very knowledgeable builder. In other words, it can happen to the best, most sophisticated builder or developer. If cost overruns can catch these guys off guard, you can bet it will sneak up on newer, less-experienced developers.

This increase in cost caught him off guard. The whole project had to be re-examined and reworked. We ended up having to get a mezzanine loan, which is like a second loan on construction in the commercial world, and the developer needed to repurpose the building as a rental building.

The point to take away from this is that even the most sophisticated borrowers in the construction space can run into trouble. So, when these companies started promoting these syndicated mortgage type products to regular investors it was very easy for the salespeople to convince average people that the projects looked really good as an investment opportunity. Let's face it, from the outside it did look really good. They also recruited a host of salespeople that were not highly trained to play ball in the big-league commercial world.

Essentially these agents, licensed as mortgage brokers, were running around the province promoting loans that they didn't fully understand. The net result? Most investors didn't fully understand. Even experienced commercial mortgage agents that have been in the industry for a long time were not up to speed in the realm of large construction condo development loans. It is a very specialized niche product.

As you can imagine many of these projects weren't properly completed. Yes, investors lost money. Mind you, some of the projects did turn out well and they were built on time and on budget. There were some great success stories as well. I am not trying to say that these situations were all bad and that they weren't completed with the belief at the beginning that all these projects were supposed to be completed properly.

As most governments do when big things hit the media, they end up creating rules and regulations around problems that existed. They try to regulate the problem and typically end up putting a larger burden on the people who are doing things the right way.

In Ontario, and in short order to be pretty much across Canada, the definition of syndicated mortgages will be spelled out in one of two ways: something called **conforming syndicated mortgages** and then something called **nonconforming or non-qualified syndicated mortgages**. Basically, the difference between the two comes down to the property type. A house, be it a residential single, duplex, triplex, up to a fourplex are considered conforming.

Typically, these transactions are easy to understand for most people. This is a good place to become familiar with the process if you're a relative novice at lending money! If you're reading this book and you're lending on a fourplex or at a triplex, whether it's by yourself or in a syndicate pool, you should be able to understand the risk of that mortgage relatively simply.

Nonconforming has a pretty broad definition, but typically it involves land deals and anything to do with construction and commercial. Any construction, not just a multi-million-dollar condo tower. If you're building a single house and you're being put in as a syndicated mortgage it is considered nonconforming property. This includes anything above a fourplex, mixed-use properties, restaurants, and commercial property.

These new rules—now in place in Ontario and shortly across the country as a whole—basically have added an immense disclosure document to try to avoid the widely publicized mistakes of the past. Make no mistake, it is extensive. Over 35 pages of disclosures, and the first 5 pages are all about scaring the pants off you to make sure that you are aware from the outset that this is a risky investment! (I wish they did this when I bought my Nortel stock!)

It's a wonder that anybody even contemplates any investments in this country with the way the government screams at you about risk, risk, risk. Have you ever stopped to wonder why they are silent about the risks that are inherent in a government investment? The government works tirelessly to convince you that you don't have any risk when you park your hard-earned money in some unknown mutual fund.

If you break it down, this type of investment has random people reviewing it, and you are ultimately investing in random companies that you have absolutely no control over. It is even hard to predict the reliability and profitability of this form of investing because there's so many variables involved. However, that's safer than letting on a piece of land in downtown Toronto, I guess. I'll get off my soapbox for now and focus on what's really important. Maybe that's my second book.

So at least the government did one thing right by saying that the level of disclosures required depends on the sophistication of the lender. If the lender investor is sophisticated, or if it's a corporation, if it's somebody that does this type of business on a regular basis, the disclosures actually are quite reasonable, and you can facilitate pretty quickly. There's also some additional rules put in place if you're not as sophisticated a lender.

If you have decided to dive into the big leagues and are intending to invest in one of these types of commercial ventures with the maximum amount of money that you can invest, I recommend looking into the disclosure details in length. Visit our website at becomingthebankbook.com for a free webinar.

I won't get into all the regulations in this book, as they vary by province. Regulations and government rules change all the time, especially when it's coming to syndicated mortgages in Canada. So, anything I write here will most likely be updated. Suffice it to say, if you're doing commercial syndicated mortgages you should be experienced, definitely ensure that you have a really good team, and can understand what you're getting into. Do your homework! Your parents were onto something when you had to complete your schoolwork before you could play video games. It comes in very handy now that you are staring into the intricacies of a new career!

I believe a syndicated mortgage on construction buildings of any kind is very different from the syndicated mortgage on a 12-unit apartment building. Real estate investors can understand the income and cash flow of a 12-unit apartment building. They can underwrite that credit risk relatively easily and you'll see I actually have a course and blog article about how to underwrite and analyze income properties.

I don't believe the type of properties in this type of syndicated mortgages carry anywhere near the same way of risk a construction project does, but I'll leave it up to you to decide what type you want to lend on, and what type of product mortgages are you looking for. Another theme that you have heard throughout the book. Ask yourself what your comfort level is. After all, the best lenders have no problem sleeping at night. They know that their money is working for them, and they have not risked more than what they feel they can handle.

One of my investors that I work with regularly got into this business by owning local warehouses and industrial properties. For him analyzing a warehouse or an industrial type of property is second nature. He can tell from the photos what type of structure it is. How long is that roof? Are the doors big enough to drive in certain types of trucks? Are the loading docks the right height? He knows all the relevant details instinctively. Just by looking at an appraisal, he's analyzed industrial properties in less than 10 minutes that would take me a few hours and maybe for you a few weeks.

So, for him investing in syndicated pools mortgages on those properties are really no risk at all because he understands the asset. However, if I brought that same investor a very high net-worth large condo construction project he would have no idea where to begin. He would have to rely 100 percent on my advice, which is great to know that he has so much trust in me, but I would be lying if I didn't say that I prefer my investors to be a little bit educated with what they lend on.

All that being said, if you do want to get into syndicated lending, start with what you're comfortable with. Sound familiar? If you ultimately are only comfortable investing in houses that's great. Stick with that. You will find success because that is what will work for you. If you don't mind going out on a limb, then dip into larger first mortgages to diversify your risk.

Decide what type of first mortgages are you looking for. Are you willing to keep your money out for a long term or would like to recoup in the short term? All the same things we discussed in the beginning of this book—what type of lender do you want to be? Only you can take the tools at your disposal, access the variables, and put on the private lender hat that fits you best.

There's also a fair number of syndicated mortgages in the second mortgage space with much higher yields at 12, 14, 16, or—heaven forbid like the story I mentioned earlier—at 24 percent interest! You can be part of whatever type of financing you want. That's what's so great about private lending. You determine the amount you lend out, at what rate, and for how long in the mortgage type of your choice.

Let's recap. Don't be scared if the broker you're working with sends you a document that says, "Warning this is a scary investment. Maybe you shouldn't be doing it. Consult your lawyer and your priest and your Rabbi and the soothsayer because it's so complicated!" The government is warning you on purpose. The aim is to really make people look at these things carefully, which is not a bad thing. However, in typical government fashion they're overreacting. Having said this, it is important, especially when it comes to construction files, to thoroughly know what you are getting into. Be familiar with the project and all relevant details pertaining to it. You will need to completely understand the project and the risk associated with it.

Due to the complexities involved, at the end of the day, I probably would recommend staying away from construction loans, at least at the beginning of your lending career.

Maybe look at smaller projects to begin with. You don't have to avoid small renovation loans that are quite common in the commercial world. The demand is out there, I see it all the time. I've seen many files come across my desk. There is a need for a few hundred thousand dollars for different reasons. Maybe they need to retrofit a building, or they need to do tenant improvements. These types of things are relatively small and easily understood versus a thirty-eight-storey concrete condo tower construction.

Summary

Chapter 6 gives an overview of the four different types of mortgages—first, second, third, and bridge loans—and the pros and cons of lending them. First mortgages have lower risk and lower interest rates, which means your return will be smaller. Second and third mortgages have higher risk and interest rates, which creates an opportunity for higher returns. Determining which type of mortgage you are willing to lend will depend on the level of risk you are willing to adopt.

Keywords

Bridge loan: "a short-term loan used until a person or company secures permanent financing or removes an existing obligation."[42]

First mortgage: "a primary lien on a property (…) (which) has priority over all other liens or claims on a property in the event of default."[43]

Second mortgage: "a type of subordinate mortgage made while an original mortgage is still in effect. In the event of default, the original mortgage would receive all proceeds from the property's liquidation until it is all paid off."[44]

Syndicated mortgage: "an arrangement in which more than one investor (i.e., lender) is involved in a loan or debt obligation secured by a mortgage."[45]

Third mortgage: "a loan wherein the principal provided by the lender is based on the value of the property and the equity that the borrower holds. Since this is the 'third' mortgage (…) it is subordinate to the first two mortgages and comes in third position behind the second mortgage."[46]

CHAPTER 7: DEFAULT MANAGEMENT: WHAT TO DO IF THEY CAN'T PAY YOU BACK

Did you know that in Canada, the overall default rate is less than 0.25 percent?[47] That is not a typo, it is under 0.25 percent, so one-quarter of 1 percent. It peaked at 0.60 percent in the '90s. If you are a data junkie, visit us at www.becometheank.ca for the complete table. Keep this in mind as we tackle this very important chapter pertaining to foreclosure and power of sale.

Let's step back for a moment and be realistic. We are not living in a perfect world and any pursuit has its drawbacks and limitations. Private lending is not immune. Yes, it would be lovely if every borrower paid back their loan on time and always had the funds to do so consistently. The vast majority of the time they do. I would be misleading you, however, if I didn't also say that sometimes, albeit rarely, they don't.

Life happens and circumstances may change. Occasionally a borrower is just not diligent enough to either pay on time or misses payments altogether. Fortunately, this is normally a rare event. It is important, however, to protect yourself in the case of default or problems with repayment of your loan. This is when default management becomes so important and helps to build the framework of your private lending business.

What Do We Mean by Default Management?

Quite simply put, **default management** is the process put in place in which we deal with borrowers when negative things may happen, and they are no longer able to pay. As I mentioned earlier, this is thankfully a rare event, but I would be irresponsible if I didn't provide you with the tools to manage such a scenario as you venture into the area of private lending.

What Is the Definition of Default?

If default management is the process put in place to deal with borrowers when negative things happen and they are no longer able to pay, then we can refer to **default** as the actual act of failing to fulfill the terms of the mortgage contract. Going into default over any loan or contract simply means the terms a particular term in a contract is not met and/or payment is late or not made.

What Are the Main Reasons for Default?

Having made the distinction between default management and actual default it makes sense for me to provide you with the main reasons why (although extremely rare, remember less than 2 percent of properties go into default) this may occur. Again, my job is to prepare you for the everyday situations you face as a lender as well as the remote and unexpected situations as well. You can never be too prepared. I will say it again because I just love the motto so darn much: Knowledge is power!

The Number One Reason for Default: Your Borrower Stops Making Payments or Is Late

This is fairly self-explanatory. You must be on top of your borrowers at all times. It is not easy to act as guardian and sheriff, but at the end of your day your primary job is to protect your investment. You are not in the business of lending out money unless that money is ultimately paid back in full, with any accumulated interest!

I will argue later in this chapter that there may be a logical and sufficient reason for your borrower to miss a payment or be late, especially at the beginning of the loan agreement. Banking issues may be an issue with the setup of a new loan for example, which is not uncommon. Having said this, you must have the appropriate measures written in the mortgage contract with your borrower to enable you to act quickly if payment is missed or late. Be proactive. It is your money. It is your investment responsibility.

What If Your Borrower Is Still Paying on Time and in Full, But the Value of the Property That You Have Leveraged Your Loan Against Has Dropped in Value?

Step 1: DON'T PANIC.
Step 2: See Step 1.

In this post-COVID-19 world with the media discussing "the housing bubble," this is a common question asked by many investors. First of all, a massive decline is very unlikely, however, it is possible. Throughout this book, we have been discussing equity and loan-to-value. I encourage you to not lend above 80 percent loan-to-value, unless in special circumstances. The other factor to consider is private lending is normally a short-term contract, one to two years. You can keep an eye on value trends and act appropriately. Also, just because the value dropped doesn't mean a loss. People still need a place to live and, in many cases, will still keep paying the mortgage.

I have decided to include this unlikely scenario on default to show you that while the standard rule of thumb of property price appreciation still applies in the vast majority of properties that private lenders will be using as collateral on their private loans, occasionally a property will depreciate in value. Although this rare circumstance does not represent a default, it does illustrate the necessity of fully researching the property you are using as collateral and knowing the specifications of the property that may leave it vulnerable to a drop in overall value.

We have already discussed how real estate almost always appreciates unlike other things such as a car or stocks on the often volatile stock market. Having said that, sometimes, albeit very rarely, a property may lose its value, leaving you with a loan that is more than the worth of the property.

This obviously will result in a loss in your money in relation to how much the property has declined in value. You will basically take a financial loss or hit.

You may be scratching your head and wondering how a property can depreciate after all the pep talk I have given you about how safe investing in real estate is. Don't get me wrong, it is very safe! Especially when compared to other forms of investment that are available to the potential investor. This will never change. However, you and I live in an imperfect world and things do happen that are beyond our control.

This is another reason why I implore you to do your research very thoroughly on the property that is serving as collateral on your loan. Go beyond the property itself and consult professionals in the real estate field concerning the area in which the property is located. What has the trend been in this particular area? What is the resale value of properties in close proximity?

You can protect yourself against a market decline somewhat by doing this extra research. This will not protect your investment against some unforeseen reason that causes the property to lessen in market value. If, however, the area declined overall in resale value then nothing can protect you from this scenario and there is no term that can be written into your contract to protect from this very rare occurrence.

A good example of a property declining in market value (albeit temporarily) is when the government steps in and enacts legislation that aims to correct an over-inflation in the market. What the government does not want to ever see is a burst in the housing bubble or real estate market. To illustrate how this has happened recently, one only has to look at the incredibly high prices of properties in some real estate properties in British Columbia, namely West Vancouver and Shaughnessy.

In both wealthy areas, housing prices had gone through the roof with upwards of a 30 percent increase per year at one point. To avoid the same housing collapse that we witnessed in 2007–2008, the Canadian government enacted the Foreign Buyers Tax in an effort to slow down the unsustainable housing prices. This Foreign Buyers Tax did affect the housing prices, bringing down property values by roughly 20 percent.

The tax also discourages some buyers (mainly buyers from Asia) from buying some of the properties for sale in these areas. Remember that this is considered a price adjustment. The housing market in these areas will increase again, albeit at not dangerous levels. Why? Because real estate is always appreciating in the long run!

There is another reason why the property may lose value (again very rarely) rather than the usual trend of appreciating consistently. This can happen if your borrower lets the property fall into a state of disrepair—if none of the fixes are done on a property to keep it in good resale form. Also, if there is an ongoing structural issue that the borrower refuses to address like a serious crack in the foundation or leak that may be causing water damage to the property.

This could also happen if the landscaping is left to a point that it is not habitable. Related to this, but not a very common scenario, the property could be used for illegal purposes that may also damage it and affect the overall market value.

In both of the above points mentioned, the underlying variable is that the borrower has not met all the terms of the contract you have negotiated (and be sure to put all of this in writing). In other words, one of the terms that you have *written* in your contract with your borrowers has failed to meet the terms of his/her contract. If this happens—don't panic, it doesn't happen very often—your borrower has defaulted and you have grounds to start a foreclosure or power of sale process.

A Couple of Ways You Can Protect Yourself

Part of your mortgage agreement prepared by your lawyer will include several clauses that will protect you as a lender. It is crucial to ensure you work with a lawyer who specializes in private lending. You can view a sample at becomingthebankbook.com.

So, it makes financial sense for them to incorporate as many protections in their mortgage contracts as possible to cover different scenarios. **THINK LIKE THE BANKS!!** I can't say this enough. You can see I like to be inspired and repeat these mottoes to be the most productive and successful I can be!

Some example clauses are:

1. Fire insurance

2. Do not demolish or renovate

3. No additional financing without permission

4. No sale without payout

5. Detailed default conditions (e.g., what scenarios trigger a default)

With these clauses, which you can include in your contract, you can protect your investment from your borrower if he or she lets the property go into a state of disrepair or uses it for illegal purposes, compromising the resale or market value of the market.

Often included in the mortgage contract to protect the lender—in your case, private lender—is a clause from a borrower that may not have any intention of keeping up the property in question. If you wish to include this clause in a contract you are drafting it should be clearly stated that the borrower has the responsibility to keep up the property and is legally obligated to do so.

If for some reason your borrower does not meet this condition of the contract, then this gives you as the private lender the right to serve notice to the borrower to make the necessary changes to the property to fall in line with what is written in his or her mortgage contract.

Often this notice is enough to rectify the problem, as unusual as it may be. If for some reason the notice does not result in the necessary upkeep of the property, then you have the right to call the loan due. It's worth considering this clause as you draft your contracts with potential borrowers. I always like to include any necessary protections in mortgage contracts to cover any eventually, however remote it may be. Again, it is your job and primary responsibility to protect your investments. Your money, your time, your best interest at heart!

Another area that could be an issue with your borrower, albeit again very rarely, is the issue of the **house insurance**. As a private lender, you are using the property in question as your collateral (two properties if you choose the blanket mortgage option) and thus you want to protect this collateral as it is critical to your overall investment.

One area that could be a potential issue is whether the property you are leveraging your loan against is **fully insured** and the **insurance is renewed** to cover the property for the duration of your loan. When you renew your mortgage (if you do) you need to ask for the insurance confirmation.

So, I recommend that you include another clause in your mortgage contract that ensures that the borrower agrees to insure the property properly during the course of the loan and does not allow for any lapse in insurance coverage. Make sure you clearly write this term in your contract and that your borrower thoroughly understands their obligations pertaining to insurance coverage. You do not want to run the risk of having any insurance coverage expire and not be renewed during the course of the mortgage loan you arrange with your borrower. This is leaving you potentially vulnerable to problems that you can easily avoid if you do your due diligence and ensure that all insurance is covered and kept up to date by your borrower. Again, write it down in your mortgage contract!

You can probably guess where I am going with this. It is logical. By now you are thinking like a private lender and putting your private lending hat on when making all decisions pertaining to your privately invested funds. What good is a property that is not insured? The potential for pitfalls and financial loss if damage occurs is real.

Trust Your Gut When Assessing Your Borrower and Late Payments

When you are starting out with a borrower in mind and thinking about structuring a loan for them, you are wise to ask yourselves the necessary questions before you put everything in writing with your borrower.

So, what do you do if the money you lent out is not being paid back? First, don't let this go on for very long! When evaluating why a borrower may be late on any given payment, clearly you need to be vigilant about determining the reason why. You also need to take it on a case-by-case basis. Ask yourself the right questions.

It comes down to how they are treating you when dealing with the issue. Is it a one time only late payment? Do they have a legitimate reason such as a mix up at the bank, or they were unexpectedly out of town, or their paycheck was late that month? The private lending business is a people-centred business after all. Interactions between you as the lender and the borrower are central in having a productive working relationship.

Having said that, if your gut is telling you that the reasons just "don't add up," then you need to be on top of the situation. Ask yourself, has it happened more than once? Do the reasons have legitimacy or do they seem to be questionable? Also ask yourself how often is a late payment occurring?

Take the example of the first payment of a mortgage you have arranged with a borrower. It is not uncommon for there to be hiccups with the first withdrawal of a payment on a new mortgage. In this instance, there is very little need to panic. Having said this, you must take immediate action and make sure you resolve the issue and get that first payment. You don't want it to get to the stage where you are running after a second payment. In other words, understand the circumstances but don't wait for this to be a pattern. Take necessary action.

Two Types of Default: Late Payments and Insufficient Funds—What Measures to Take

There are two types of default when you are lending out through private channels. The first area of default is the **late payment**. The second area of default to consider is non-sufficient funds (**NSF**) **payments**.

It is also important to step back for a minute and truly encompass all the areas that potentially can fall under the broad term "default." Yes, the late or missed payment is the one that will be the most likely scenario if you were to encounter problems with your client's ability to pay back your privately lent funds. There are other areas that one can potentially run into problems and represent a form of default on your mortgage loan.

1. **Insurance unpaid:** If a borrower fails to make an insurance payment on the loan you have negotiated with him or her, then this also represents a form of going into default on your loan. Take ac-

tion immediately as it is within your means to do so based on the parameters of the loan you negotiated with your borrower.

2. **Not renewing the mortgage**: If the borrower fails to renew the mortgage on time this is also a form of default and must also be addressed and rectified immediately.

3. **Letting property conditions go:** The property must be well-maintained and letting it go into disrepair can also be classified as a form of default and again must be addressed sooner rather than later.

4. **Taxes unpaid on property**: This is also an area to keep a close eye on. Any unpaid taxes must be tracked and paid immediately as this represents going into default as well.

5. **First mortgage goes into default:** If your borrower is found to have gone into default on a first mortgage owing on the same property that you have lent out a second or even third mortgage on, this can be a red flag. There may be a ripple effect, potentially ending up with a default on the other mortgages on the property you are using as leverage in your loan to your borrower.

Don't forget to add your NSF fee. This can represent a large source of revenue!

We touched on the potential issue of what to do if there is a late payment. After determining the possible reasons why this occurred and carefully assessing what exactly the borrower is relaying to you about the issue, you may need to allocate for the possibility that there may be one initial late payment.

You can forgive the late payment *but* must ensure that it is properly and promptly made as soon as possible. When I say forgive, I mean accept the circumstances that caused the late payment. This does not mean let the late payment or missed payment slide. Be understanding and then take steps to get your payment ASAP.

If this payment is not made or it looks as though this might be representative of a pattern in your client, you must take the necessary punitive steps right away. Remember one late payment can be explained and quickly ratified. Nip it in the bud immediately to not be in the position of two missed or late payments! It is absolutely necessary to take quick action and requires immediate punitive action.

The Mortgage Payment Check Bounced. What Exactly Should You Do?

This second potential scenario is far more worrisome from a private lender's perspective. In a default payment, the funds are not there, and payments are missed altogether for any given month. Insufficient funds and missed payments represent a red flag and must be addressed. Don't forget that in the area of default management you must **decide at the outset what punitive measures you will implement** in the rare event that the borrower's checks do not go through.

Good news. Remember the element of control I hammered home to you in Chapter 1? This real element of control comes to play in all areas of private lending, including how you decide to manage borrowers that go into default. When lending privately, you can determine how much you lend, the method by which you lend, as well as determining the rate you wish to charge on money lent out.

Don't Forget to Determine What Default Charges You Will Enforce

By the same token, if a borrower goes into default by being late more than once in his or her payments and especially if a check bounces, you can determine what **default charges** you will charge. You decide the rate and make these charges known to the borrower at the outset as you determine the parameters of the mortgage loan.

Default charges are really at the heart of the punitive measures you can use to enforce payment while protecting your investments. In fact, some private lenders have made a considerable amount of money from default charges alone on money they have lent out!

The late charges and penalty fees factor into the overall return on your investment. The steeper the penalty charge, the more unlikely the borrower will risk late or missed payments. If, however, payments are not made, you will still profit in the short term.

I have known private lenders who have deliberately decided to let late payments and missed payments go. By overlooking these default payments private lenders have made a small fortune by collecting penalty fees and default charges from their clients.

> Loan Amount $30,000
> Payment: $300 per month
> NSF fee: $395
>
> This client missed 6 of 12 payments. We tried to work with them, even to the point of calling and emailing a few days in advance. We waived a few NSF fees to help them catch up, all of which didn't matter. There was a LOT of equity in the home, so there was no risk, just annoyance. However, the lender at first was stressed out until I explained the rate of return that he was getting. In my opinion, structuring deals this way with big back-end fees or hidden renewal fees in hopes people will default is not good business. These fees are meant to be a deterrent, not a profit source for most lenders. Your reputation as a lender will follow you, so ensure you act in the most ethical ways.

Let it be on the record that despite some private lenders taking this route, I am not a big fan of relying on default charges to make a large amount of money on your investment. Rather, I feel that it is imperative that you keep on top of your investments. Do not give your borrowers a long leash.

Keep in mind when dealing with potential issues with your borrowers that this is a business deal, and you are not stepping in as a friend. You have entered into a **business contract** and measures must be articulated up front with the borrower and **enforced when necessary**.

Two Choices: Foreclosure or Power of Sale

The borrower has been late more than once on his or her payment. Maybe things are worse. The borrower has missed two payments in a row. What if the borrower has stopped paying at all? You are now officially in default territory. You have been charging the fees to the borrower that you had determined at the outset of the mortgage loan. Now what?

Now you are faced with two options depending on what province you are in. **Foreclosure** or **power of sale**.

The Foreclosure Process

In foreclosure, the lender is able to take title and become the OWNER of the property versus just having the right to possess and sell the property. With foreclosure, the lender must start a court proceeding and sue the borrower and must wait for the courts to issue judgment.

This requires much more legal work to be processed by the lender's lawyers. Once the foreclosure is finished, the lender takes title to the property, and the former homeowner is not entitled to any future profit from the sale of the property. However, the lender also cannot sue the borrower for any future loss. Since this has the potential to strip equity away from borrowers, the courts have traditionally been wary of this process in Ontario.

The province you are lending in will have specific rules and timing. For example, in Saskatchewan there are some very specific rules around lending to farms that are considered a "homestead."

Power of Sale Process

In a power of sale, the mortgage lender is able to evict the property occupants and sell the property if the borrower is in default of the mortgage. It is important to note that the lender is required to sell the property at fair market value. You CANNOT sell it at a deep discount. After the property is sold, the former homeowner has the right to any profit from the sale after deducting debt repayment and fees.

All the excess profit from the sale goes to the owner of the home. Lenders typically do not earn additional profit from completing the power of sale other than a WACK load of fee. We would much rather the borrower pay off their debt than sell the property under power of sale.

One of the benefits of power of sale is that it is a much faster process than foreclosure and requires less involvement from the court system. Most power of sales can be completed within six months, but a foreclosure can take over a year or even more to complete.

You can also go after the borrowers for any losses you incur should you have any.

In order to navigate either territory, I strongly recommend that you retain the services of a lawyer who is well versed in this area of the mortgage process. Don't use lawyers on an ad hoc basis or rely on legal advice from colleagues or friends or, for heaven's sake, SOCIAL MEDIA! Ensure that whatever lawyer you choose understands the intricacies and legalities of foreclosures and power of sales. He or she should encounter this area often and be considered an expert in this area.

Don't be concerned about the costs involved in hiring a lawyer in the event of a power of sale or foreclosure. Yes, in the unlikely event of a foreclosure, you will be bearing any associated cost that results from taking punitive action.

However, you are the one that will get any equity that has been built up in the property first, rather than the borrower. There are inevitable costs involved in forcing a foreclosure on a particular property. Having said that, the equity owing on the property will most likely more than make up for any potential losses incurred in the costs of foreclosure. In essence, the risk and the reward are borne by the lender in the event of foreclosure.

A Quick Math Lesson on Default Sales

Home value: $500,000

You lend $400,000 1st mortgage

Loan-to-value: 80%

Rate: 7.5% (monthly compounding)

Payment: $2,500

Property taxes: $5,000 per year

The borrower pays well for the first few months, then stops paying and you are forced to do a power of sale. Since the home will most likely be in not the best shape you will need to clean it up and it never sells for the same price as an owner-occupied home.

Sale price due to power of sale: $485,000

Real estate fees: 5%, $24,250 + tax

Six months payments $2,500 x 6 = $15,000 (assuming it takes six months for the courts, sale time and possession)

Property tax arrears: $2,500

Insurance cost: $2,000

Repairs and inspections: $10,000 (this could be a lot more)

Legal fees: $10,000

Net sale proceeds: $421,250

Less mortgage principle: $400,000

Other chargers to borrower: $10,000

Net cash to borrower: $11,250

Now if you had a second mortgage instead of first, you would need to also make all the payments on the first mortgage and pay the legal fees of the first mortgage lender. This is why it is so important to keep control when a borrower started defaulting. The big banks have VERY expensive lawyers.

If you have been a diligent student and completed all the homework on your mortgage deal and the lending process, there should be no problem recouping all of your investment in the event of default. It is imperative that when carrying out this lending homework that you do not over-leverage your client. If this is the case, you should recoup all of your capital, all of your fees, and all the interest made on the mortgage loan when or if the property goes into foreclosure or you take power of sale on that property.

What Are the Key Differences Between Foreclosure and Power of Sale?

Power of Sale

The best way to describe this term is when one is taking the **right to sell the property**. You have been given the power to sell a home or property. In the event of power of sale, the homeowner still owns the home but you, in the capacity of the lender, now have the legal right to sell it.

The homeowner at this point will be served with an eviction notice and you, as the lender, will take over possession of the home or property. You can now sell the property. This process is quite quick and straightforward, which is one of the main benefits of the method of power of sale.

Note, however, that any profit made on the sale of the property legally goes back to the property owner or borrower. Another benefit of power of sale is that you avoid lengthy court proceedings with this method when dealing with lender default. The whole process can take as little as a few months at little cost to you as the lender.

Foreclosure

Foreclosure differs from power of sale in several respects. The most significant difference between the method of power of sale and foreclosure is that when a property goes into foreclosure **you take over ownership of the property**. You are responsible for all potential gains on the property as well as all liabilities.

Foreclosure typically involves lengthy court proceedings to carry out and can be costly. When taking over ownership of the property you are entitled to keep any profit made, but be aware that you will not have the legal right to sue the borrower for any shortfalls.

Because you now have ownership over the property there is the obvious upside of retaining any profits made on the sale of the property, but you are not without risk as you are now on the hook for any liabilities associated with that particular property. Ask yourself if the potential for increased profit outweighs the risk involved.

As you can see, the most significant difference between the process of power of sale and foreclosure are:

1. The involvement of the courts

In the event that you are forced to start foreclosure proceedings (sometimes referred to as judicial sale), you must do so **through the courts**. It becomes a legal process involving lawyers and the court's approval. In other words, you must make an application with the courts to start the foreclosure process.

In the event of a power of sale, the court role is minimized. This becomes an attractive option as it is fairly straightforward and certainly a faster process than is often the case with the process of foreclosure. You, as a private lender, can go after your borrower and demand the sale of the property.

This also relates to the costs involved for you as a private lender. In the foreclosure process, as a private lender you will have to incur all the legal cost associated with it. However, you will be entitled to any equity in the property, which should more than cover the court and legal fees.

In a power of sale, as a private lender you will be taking over rights to the property and taking on the job of selling the property yourself. Your costs for real estate fees in addition to any associated legal fees will come out of the proceeds from the sale of the house.

2. How the proceedings are initiated

The second major distinction to make between the process of foreclosure and power of sale is just how you, as a private lender, will go about starting or initiating the proceedings. In the case of power of sale, you will be sending a notice directly to your borrower informing that you will be starting the power of sale process as your borrower has been found to be default. He or she has, in other words, not reached every term of the mortgage contract.

In the event of a foreclosure, or judicial sale, you will have to apply to the court asking for permission for the court to start proceedings and you will require the services of a real estate lawyer.

3. The time that each process takes

It stands to reason that because each process differs in that one involves the courts, and by extension lawyers, while the other does not, the time the process will take will differ considerably. As you might have guessed, now that you are well versed in many aspects of the private lending process, you can easily ascertain that the foreclosure process takes considerably more time because of having to make an application directly to the courts.

This is always a timely process, and the timeline is determined by the courts. With the process of power of sale, you as the lender will not be required to go through the courts. So, the process is by nature a much quicker one.

State or Provincial Differences When Dealing with Default

As we progress through the ins-and-outs of default and the processes to deal with it, keep in mind that you are restricted by what process you end up using in the unlikely event that your borrower goes into default. This is because depending on what state or province you are in, the process is determined by the state or provincial government by which method lenders can utilize to deal with default. You will have to adhere to the default rules in the province in which you are privately lending your funds.

Also be aware that what method you end up taking in the event of default is also largely determined by what measures are most often used in the state or province. For example, in Ontario where my private lending deals originate, it is very rare to resort to foreclosure.

By contrast, in some states and provinces foreclosure is the only measure that one can use when dealing with default. Usually, if foreclosure is the measure used most often, very specific rules have been put into place pertaining to properties that fall in foreclosure. Do your homework, research what rules and measures are in place in your province, and make sure to articulate what measures will be used to your customers in the event that they do not meet the payment conditions.

Here is a brief outline of what process is used by provinces in my home country of Canada. I urge you to do your homework and make sure you are aware of the intricacies of the steps that you may need to follow in the remote case you need to look into initiating proceedings with your borrower.

Ontario

I am starting with Ontario because this is where my business is based and all of my commercial and private real estate dealings transpire. One does not need to look any further than the Ontario Mortgages Act to illustrate the process that you must follow when tackling the issue of default.

In Ontario, and stated in the Ontario Mortgages Act, a lender will be utilizing the **power of sale** process when dealing with a borrower who has defaulted on terms, or a term of the mortgage contract that you have negotiated and the borrower has signed. In this case you must keep in mind that there are several steps involved before you can legally take possession of the property and attempt to sell it.

Allow for 15 days: Once your borrower has missed a payment or is substantially late or has broken another mortgage term such as failure to pay insurance on the property, the Ontario Mortgage Act requires that you provide your borrower 15 days to try to rectify the situation and before you can exercise power of sale.

Note that you must always include a power of sale clause in your mortgage contract to allow you to start the process in the case of borrower default. If you do not include this provision in your contract with your borrower, then you will have to resort to what is referred to as a statutory power of sale. Statutory power of sale does not happen very often in Ontario because including a power of sale provision in a mortgage contract, whether through a big bank, through a commercial mortgage broker, or negotiated privately is considered a crucial term to *always* include in your written mortgage contract. If you have not allowed for the power of sale provision, then you can still go after the property in question, but it will take an extra 10 days to complete the process.

Once you have passed the 15-day period after a term of your mortgage contract has not been met, you are now entitled to send a letter to your borrower. This letter is referred to as a notice, specifically a **notice of sale**. The notice of sale letter will specify that the borrower has gone into default and that the borrower has a **redemption period** to try to rectify the situation by making up any missed payments or meeting the term of the contract that had not been met.

The redemption period is 35 days in Ontario. Remember if you over-looked adding a power of sale provision in your contract and are utilizing the statutory power of sale, you must allow your borrower 45 days to meet all terms of your mortgage contract. It is only after the redemption period that you can now legally sell the property. You can sell this property in a number of ways, including on auction.

I recommend using the professional services of a real estate agent to help you sell the property quickly. Remember you have incentive—your money is tied up in this property and in order to pay off all the associated fees, the equity built up in the property will be covering your costs!

Remember that the best way to avoid any problems down the road is to hire a recommended real estate lawyer that has plenty of experience drafting mortgage contracts. You will also need a third-party appraisal.

British Columbia

British Columbia's methods for dealing with mortgage default differ con-siderably from Ontario on several fronts. The most glaring difference is that the method used to handle the issue of default is foreclosure (judicial sale) as opposed to power of sale. That means that the courts will be deter-mining the timing of the process and will be involved from start to finish.

In BC, the protections for the borrower or homeowner are quite exten-sive. The court is involved all the way through the process, and you must have everything approved by the court. The process of selling the property is also overseen by the courts. The court will determine the purchase price and be involved through the whole resale process of the property.

Nova Scotia

In Nova Scotia, the rules dictate that you can use both processes—foreclo-sure and power of sale. In other words, depending on circumstances either method is deemed acceptable in dealing with default. Make sure to hire a real estate lawyer to help you navigate the system pertaining to mortgage default.

New Brunswick

When it comes to the particularities of the laws pertaining to mortgage default, things have changed from what they were originally. Before 1982, this province used to use both foreclosure and power of sale, depending on the circumstances pertaining to a particular property. After 1982, the province chose to use power of sale. It was deemed a less complicated, less expensive, and faster process than foreclosure.

Alberta, Manitoba, and Quebec

Unlike Ontario, these provinces use the traditional process of foreclosure to resolve default when it comes to mortgages. This, of course, means that the courts are involved, and the timing is determined by the courts.

Prince Edward Island and Newfoundland

In these two provinces, similar to Ontario, the method of choice when dealing mortgage default is by power of sale. This means that after the redemption period expires, you can take back the property and resell it by the method you choose. Remember this is only easy and timely if you had your mortgage contract drafted by a real estate lawyer and more importantly added the power of sale clause to your contract.

Don't Forget That There Are Other Forms of Mortgage Default Beyond a Missed or Late Payment

Note that there are other forms of default that go beyond missed payments:

1. **Failure to pay property taxes** represents a form of default.

2. **Failure to pay insurance** on the property.

3. **Having leans on a property** may fall in the default territory as well. Make sure to make sure this does not become an issue!

4. A **first mortgage on a property in default can also trigger a second mortgage default** as a result. Look at the payment history of the first mortgage before committing.

An Often-Overlooked Third Measure to Tackle Default

Power of sale and foreclosure are the standard methods for handling mortgage default. There is also a third process for handling default that is not as well known. Keep in mind that this method for handling default is used very rarely in Canada. As a result, it is unlikely that you will be choosing this method. Having said this, in the United States this default process is used quite often.

Quit Claim Deeds

In this process, the owner of the property signs over the ownership rights. The owner will sign over any interest they have in the property. The obvious advantage to this rarely-used process is by the nature of the owner signing over ownership, the process is considerably faster than the other methods of power of sale and foreclosure. It is also, by extension, less expensive to handle the sticky issue of default. When it is used, it tends to be predominantly used by spouses in the event of divorce.

Have All Your Ducks in a Row to Handle the Unexpected

You may be scratching your head and asking whether the risk of default is worth the investment of your funds with a potential borrower. I am here to say once again: YES. The rewards far outweigh the risks.

This aptly applies to the area of default. You can protect yourself from any number of possible but highly unlikely scenarios. Make sure to add the necessary protections in writing in your mortgage contracts and have an experienced real estate lawyer look over your final contracts with a fine-tooth comb. And above all else, be confident in the knowledge that any risk to you is minimal compared to the roller coaster ride of the stock market or having the big banks dictate the terms of your investments!

Have your plan of attack. Line up the best people to help you enforce if necessary. Know your deal inside out. Decide on which method to use if the property goes into default. Include all punitive measures in your mortgage contract and clearly outline what you define as default as it relates to a specific deal. Research the borrowing history of your customer.

Protect your investment! Sounds logical right? Yes, but until you have crossed your t's and dotted your i's your job is not done. Only when you have a complete understanding of the punitive measures available to you and you have the legal representation to back it up, coupled with all measures clearly outlined in a mortgage contract, can you be assured that your investment is fully protected.

Summary

Chapter 7 covers what to do if your borrower defaults on their loan, some common reasons why this happens, and some ways to protect yourself as a lender. It also discusses some legal specificities to be aware of across different regions in Canada.

Keywords

Default: "the failure to repay a debt," including a mortgage.[48]

Default management: methods used to mitigate the damage of a defaulted loan, including reinstatement and forbearance.[49]

Foreclosure: "the legal process by which a lender attempts to recover the amount owed on a defaulted loan by taking ownership of the mortgaged property and selling it."[50]

Power of sale: "a clause written into a mortgage note authorizing the mortgagee to sell the property in the event of default in order to repay the mortgage debt."[51]

CHAPTER 8: CRASH COURSE ON CREDIT SCORES

We all know that the big banks are quite rigid in the requirements they set in place when considering various loan applications. In Chapter 2, I talked about how to think like a bank.

Mastering this mindset probably represents one of the most important ingredients in the recipe for success as a private lender. A little bit of sugar, a little bit of spice, and a whole lot of the right mindset for private lending success!

Even though you ultimately set the rules and the terms for your mortgage agreement as a private lender, you would be wise to take a page from the playbook of the big banks. Make sure the conditions that you have decided upon in your real estate investment are clear and articulated in writing to your customer. Just as in the rare event of default, you have made sure all the punitive measures are to be put in print in your contract.

You should also decide what criteria you will be using to assess a potential deal *before* entering into a private lending relationship. Be clear in your mind what minimum conditions need to be met by a new client and provide these conditions in writing to be sure the potential client is also clear what conditions need to be met and upheld.

This leads us to some of the most important criteria to look for when considering entering into a private lending contract with a new client. Top of the list: the **credit score.** When potential clients are turning to traditional lenders, namely the banks, one of the first things that is determined is the overall credit score of the client. Remember, banks ultimately want to lend out as little as possible with the lowest level of risk.

By assessing a client's credit score the banks are essentially analyzing what degree of risk any given individual represents when it comes to recouping their money. The credit score in the lending business tells the story. It represents essentially a snapshot of the lending history of an individual and his or her reliability and consistency in terms of repayment.

How Is My Credit Score Calculated?

The reporting agencies—Equifax, TransUnion, and Equifax—have not provided mortgage professionals with the exact way in which they come up with your ultimate credit score. However, it is without a doubt that there are specific criteria that they are analyzing. This criterion forms that basis of the calculations that they ultimately make. Below is a brief outline of the elements that are assessed when determining an individual's overall credit score.

Payment History
- Approximately 35 percent of the score
- Account payment details
- Presence of adverse public records or collection items
- Severity of delinquency
- Number of past due items
- Date of recent collection, public records, and past due indicators
- Amount past due on delinquent or collection accounts

Utilization
- Approximately 30 percent of the score
- All accounts
- Specific accounts

- Number of accounts with balances
- Utilization of some revolving credit lines

Length of Credit History

- Approximately 15 percent of the score
- Time since account open date

Mix of Credit Products

- Approximately 10 percent of the score
- Number and types of accounts
- Prevalence and recent trade related data

Inquiries

- Up to 7 percent of the score
- Volume/type of recent inquiries

The majority of people have no idea how the tiniest little hiccup can affect their credit score. This most likely stems from the fact that not everyone has taken the time to inquire about what are the determining variables that are used to obtain the credit score. You should be very aware of what your credit score represents from a personal standpoint.

This knowledge is invaluable because as a future private lender you will be analyzing credit reports and have to obtain the understanding of why your borrower has the credit score that he or she has. What variables have affected your borrower's score? How has the borrower managed their credit? What is the overall credit worthiness of your borrower?

You Should Be Very Interested in Your Client's Overall Credit Score

Factoring in credit score along with other valuable criteria is vital in putting together a solid mortgage package. Taking into account credit score falls into the category of laying the groundwork for a solid and relatively low-risk mortgage deal.

It is very important to differentiate between the **credit score** and the **credit history**. These are often confused and in actuality are two different measures in a borrower's overall credit worthiness.

Credit Scores

Think of the credit score as the final numerical summary after factoring in all the criteria that goes into the credit report. After looking at: credit reports.

Credit Report

It is logical that just as the credit score stems from analyzing the credit worthiness of an individual, the credit report is a detailed listing of these criteria. A complete history of how an individual has handled their credit as well as any delinquency that may have occurred. It is a very detailed report that gives an overall picture of an individual's overall credit worthiness.

Determining Whether Dips in Credit Scores Are a Reason for Concern

Put your analytical skills to use now. After making this crucial distinction between the overall credit score of your borrower and his or her credit history or report you must use your judgment as to whether you determine that the borrower represents a risk when lending to. Just as in the event of default, you should look at each credit score on a case-by-case basis within the context of what life events may have transpired.

Has your client gone through a tough divorce? Was there a job loss that impacted overall credit score? Was there a health issue that may have affected income and ability to pay bills as a result? You are looking for an overall pattern of consistency in the ability to pay back debts on time and in full. Life can, and ultimately does, throw some fairly jaw dropping curveballs that can throw a client off their solid credit course.

Just as you are looking at the history of credit payments, you are also looking at the client's overall financial history. Be aware that one of the reasons clients come to you in the first place is because they may have run into stumbling blocks when trying to obtain a loan from the banks or other traditional lenders. Circumstances, perhaps beyond their control, may have affected their credit, preventing them from securing a loan through a big bank.

Be vigilant. Do your research on the reasons why their credit may be damaged. Don't overlook these clients. Look at the whole picture. Has there been a default on their first mortgage? Do they have considerable assets to secure your mortgage loan against? Do they have considerable savings?

By now you are getting an understanding of what questions to ask to determine whether the possible deal has the potential to be a lucrative one with relatively low risk. Just as in default situations, look for patterns to determine likely outcomes. Past behaviour is always the best predictor of future behaviour, especially when it comes to payment history. Keep in mind that you are a private lender. If your borrower's credit was outstanding and did not have any issues, your borrower would be negotiating mortgage terms with a bank and not with you.

More on Credit Reports

Let's take a moment to break down the various elements of the credit report and truly understand what the overall credit score is actually indicating. As a successful private lender, you will need to be able to pull the relevant information from the report and be able to analyze it correctly. This skill and knowledge set will help you enormously when approaching a new client.

Knowing what to look for and analyzing credit trends with a client as well as pinpointing red flags will help you to determine whether you deem your potential client to have met the financial criteria that you have set out. This, of course, impacts your assessment of the overall risk that any given client may represent in a mortgage agreement with you.

The best way to look at the credit bureau is that it represents a story. What does it tell you about your potential client? Think of it as a character profile. In Canada, the actual FICO score, or credit score, is generated by Equifax. TransUnion also generates a slightly different credit score. There are two credit bureaus in Canada: **Equifax** and **TransUnion**. The credit bureau is essentially a financial bulletin board.

It serves as a method to post financial information for each individual to create an overall picture of that individual's credit history. I strongly encourage everyone considering lending out money privately to check his or her own credit score. It's a great way to get an idea of what information is posted on the credit board and become familiar with what to look for when you are required to evaluate your client's overall financial record.

```
CB Canada Inc.        Credit Bureau View    May-13-2021 08:47:02 AM EST
                      Dan Homeowner          Great Lender Inc.
                                             1111 Any Road
                                             Smalltown, Ontario
                                             X4X 3Z9 Canada

Credit Bureau Report

USER REF. PLENDER          THIS FORM PRODUCED BY CB CANADA INC.       P   1
MULTIPLE FILES INDICATOR: 0
CB CANADA INC.AND AFFILIATE BUREAUS-REFER CONSUMER INQUIRIES TO 1-888-123-4567

   FN 00-0000000-00-000 UN 0111111111   05/13/21               PG01

AML ASSIST (SUBJECT)
*****************
AML HEADER
*****************
SINGLE SOURCE HIT          : Y
DUAL SOURCE HIT            : N
WATERFALL PROCESSED        : N
SINGLE SOURCE DECISION     : N
DUAL SOURCE DECISION       :
ORIGIN OF CREDIT FILE      : CANADA
CREDIT FILE CREATED DATE   : 1982/01/01
NUMBER OF TRADES ON FILE   : 013
OLDEST TRADE ON FILE
OPEN DATE                  : 2000/02/24
UNIQUE NUMBER (CID)        : 0000001111
INPUT NAME                 : HOMEOWNER,DAN,

INPUT ADDRESS              : 11 ANYWHERE DRIVE,ON,X1Y 2D2

INPUT DOB                  : 1962/01/01

*****************
AML SINGLE SOURCE
*****************
LAST NAME MATCH            : Y
FIRST NAME MATCH           : Y
MIDDLE NAME MATCH          : X
SUFFIX MATCH               : X
CIVIC MATCH                : Y
STREET NAME MATCH          : Y
CITY MATCH                 : N
POSTAL CODE MATCH          : Y
PROVINCE MATCH             : Y
DATE OF BIRTH MATCH        : P
FIRST FORMER ADDRESS MATCH : N
SECOND FORMER ADDRESS MATCH : N
NAME AS REPORTED           : HOMEOWNER,DAN,

AKA NAME AS REPORTED1      :

AKA NAME AS REPORTED2      :

AKA NAME AS REPORTED3      :

AKA NAME AS REPORTED4      :

                        Page 1 of 5
```

Sample first page of a Credit Bureau Report. To see the full report turn to the appendix in the back of the book.

Different financial institutions that are members of the credit bureau, such as the major banks or billers, will provide credit information to be posted through Equifax or TransUnion. The credit bureaus represent the custodians of the financial bulletin board.

It is not uncommon for individuals to want to lay blame with the credit bureaus if they feel that the financial information posted misrepresents them. This is actually laying blame with the wrong party. Each financial institution, whether it be your bank or utility company, will provide the credit bureaus with what they have concluded is the correct financial information pertaining to any given individual.

This does not mean that an individual is prevented from contesting information that he or she may feel misrepresents them. The point to be made here is that the credit bureau represents an agreed-upon platform in which to provide detailed credit information from a number of financial sources.

I can think of an example in my past experience with the credit bureau that illustrated my point. A few years ago, I encountered a hiccup in what was being posted to my financial board, so to speak. Thankfully, in this particular instance, it did not affect my overall FICO score or show up as any major financial delinquency. Nevertheless, it had the potential to impact me in terms of how a financial institution may have perceived me.

Somehow, one of the financial institutions that showed up on my Equifax report would automatically update my home address to my office address. So, I was repeatedly forced to go through the hoops with providing my driver's licence and proof of address to rectify the mix up in the system.

You may be asking why this would impact things at all on a financial level. The answer is that if someone was "reading" my financial record they may look at the change of address every few months and perceive this as a sign of instability. Questions may arise in their mind such as why is he moving so often?

Is there a problem in terms of paying the mortgage? Are things unstable on the job front? These questions that result from what appeared to be a frequent change of address may in turn impact my ability to apply for a loan or apply for refinancing.

Keep in mind that the credit report serves the purpose of painting an overall picture of an individual's financial history. The picture that was being painted in this instance did not capture the reality of my living situation and overall stability. It is important to note here that not only do past addresses and an individual's creditors show up on standard credit reports but so does one's employment details.

Employment details help to round out the financial picture as well, so I recommend studying this section of a given credit report when researching a client's credit background. I would say that although the actual FICO score is relevant, at the end of the day it is of less importance than the other aspects we have mentioned. Many things can affect a credit score, and this should not deter you from lending money if the other variables are in place. I can't stress this point enough: look at the whole picture before determining how risky a particular client may seem to you.

How do you put together all these pieces of the financial puzzle as a private lender? You are looking for red flags. Cross-reference. Does your borrower's employment history and job history match the application? You are looking for patterns in payment history. You are looking for employment details. You are looking for possible cases of fraud or misrepresentation. Ask yourself if any late or missed payments looked to be an isolated event for example.

This brings us back to the impact of unforeseen life changes temporarily impacting FICO scores and overall credit. Although clearly important and not to be overlooked don't forget that FICO scores can be affected in different ways. At the end of the day, as a private lender you are painting an overall picture about your future client.

The credit check is thrown into the mix along with the other criteria that you have thoughtfully established as benchmarks in a mortgage deal. Bottom line: use the credit report as a guide, the credit score as a beacon, and then use your intuition and gut as the final determinant when deciding to enter into a private lending relationship with any given client.

Credit Ratings Broken Down

It is certainly worth your while to be familiar with the various credit ratings that you will be seeing on your potential borrower's credit report. First, it is important to make a distinction between various categories that the two major reporting companies in Canada, Equifax and TransUnion, use to classify different loans, credit cards, and debts.

I know that you are going to analyze these variables because I have instructed you to! Why read the book and not heed the advice!

O: Open accounts. These are loans that have a specified time period for the borrower to pay back. They literally stay open until paid in full. An example to illustrate this type of loan is a student loan.

I: Instalment Loans. These are loans that are set up for the borrower to pay back in equal instalments. A good example of this type of account is a store card when you are paying off furniture in equal instalments for a designated time period. Another obvious example would be a car loan that is paid in instalments until paid off during a designated time frame.

R: Revolving loans. This refers to most commonly credit cards or lines of credit. The definition of a revolving loan is one where once your borrower pays off a portion or all of the money owing, the money is available again for use. It revolves as you use and pay it off.

Let's Break It Down Even Further: R-Ratings Classified

As you may know, the revolving credit rating on credit reports has been assigned a credit rating. This credit rating is very important for you to analyze when determining the overall credit worthiness of your borrower. This is considered by lenders and mortgage professionals as a good indicator of how reliable your borrower may be in paying back his or her loans.

Of course, life happens. We already have established this indisputable fact. Having said this, keep in mind what you're doing when analyzing a credit report. You are trying to paint an overall picture of your borrower. You are looking for payment trends and behaviours related to the reliability of paying creditors. After all you are in the position of the lender now.

You need to be aware of what all lenders look for in their potential clients. It is up to you to assess whether your funds will be in good hands and be paid on time and in full, with any interest that has incurred in these funds.

So, What Do Each of the Revolving Credit Ratings Mean, Exactly?

R1: This indicates the borrower is up to date with their payments, credit cards, bills, etc.

R2: This indicates your borrower is 30 days late in their payment.

R3: This indicates that your borrower is 60 days late in their payment(s).

R4: This indicates that your borrower is 90 days late in their payments(s).

R5: This indicates that your borrower is 120 days late in their payment(s).

R6: This indicates that your borrower has stopped making payments (usually not used).

R7: This indicates that the borrower has been written off or is in credit counselling.

R8: This indicates that the process of repossession has begun.

R9: This indicates bad debt write off.

You will frequently see errors on credit bureaus. For example, a customer is a consumer proposal so the account should be coded as a R7 but it reports as R9. Don't get caught in these small errors. Regardless, the debt is in default.

Having a thorough understanding of your potential client's credit score can be invaluable. Knowing the credit score will play a huge role in determining whether you will lend to someone.

Before finishing this chapter, I want to also define what a credit score is to help you in your credit evaluation of future borrowers. Simply put, a credit score that is generated by Equifax or TransUnion. It is a score that ranges from 300 to 900 with 300 representing the least creditworthy. At the highest end, the beacon score of 900 represents the best possible score in terms of the reliability in terms of paying on time and in full to creditors as well as being deemed the most creditworthy. In the broker industry, we refer to a credit score of 900 as the Unicorn score. I have only seen it twice in 25 years.

Evaluating Credit Dips—Is This a Pattern?

We talked about looking at every potential mortgage deal on a case-by-case basis. Carefully evaluating all the criteria, you have set out as being important to you. We have also examined what a credit report reveals about a potential client as well as determining the level of priority you will give to a potential client's overall credit score. I will take this a step further and help you determine if a series of credit black marks represent an overall trend that negatively reflects on your client or if there is a plausible explanation.

I don't have to look much further than a past client that approached me to obtain a mortgage. He had run into stumbling blocks in qualifying for a mortgage and as it turns out this was directly related to a couple of black marks on his Equifax report. I analyzed his report, and it was revealed that he had been several months late on two separate credit cards during a specific time period. Other than this blip on his credit report everything else was exemplary.

In this specific case, my client had left the country to go to the Middle East to care for his mom. On a regular basis he had automatic payments set up to pay credit cards on time, but he had unfortunately overlooked two cards. He was abroad for over two months and when he returned his credit rating had dropped. Two credit card companies had reported to Equifax that they had not received payment. Before this occurred, by all measures my client had a perfect credit history which he had been vigilant to protect.

It was incumbent on me to look at the overall picture of his credit worthiness. By tracing back in time over his credit history I discovered that he had no other red flags or black marks on his credit report. What happened to my client perfectly illustrates how important it is to know what to look for in a credit report. I strongly encourage you to look at the whole financial picture when you are determining the financial stability of a client. It is important that you don't just focus on the credit score.

To play devil's advocate, I have also had clients who are quick to try to talk their way out of credit discrepancies and late or missed payments. I can buy the idea that one missed cell phone payment could happen to anyone depending on other influences that may have come to play. Two late or missed payments is highly questionable. Three demonstrates a pattern of unreliability that should alert you to potential problems when deciding to loan out your money to them.

I have had clients give me the most creative excuses to explain less-than-positive checkmarks on their credit report. I have become very adept at reading when someone is being honest rather than just trying to cover up a lazy history of payments. Trust your gut. What is this information really saying about the likelihood that a possible client is going to pay back on time when taking out a loan from you?

The great takeaway from this short and sweet chapter is that along with being vigilant about being on top of a late or missed payment as well as having all contingency plans in place to handle a potential default, you should also take into consideration the context of your borrower. Look at what life circumstances may have conspired to cause a blip in their creditworthiness. Borrowers are not just a credit score, so factor in mitigating factors and then make your decision in regard to his/her overall credit reliability.

They're your funds to lend, your borrower to select, and your questions to ask. Base your decision on knowledge you have learned by researching your borrower. Get a feeling for him/her and a long and broad picture of their reliability when it comes to repaying loans. The ball is in your court. Plan for the unexpected but look at all mitigating circumstances when it comes to selecting your borrower and lending out your hard-earned funds.

The Credit Takeaway

In essence, when you are assessing your borrower in terms of whether they are a good candidate to privately lend to, you will be looking at several different factors. All of these factors come to play to create an overall financial picture of your potential borrower.

Ask yourself the right questions. What is the beacon score calculated for your potential borrower? What revolving credit rating has been assigned to him or her? Has there been a consistent pattern of paying on time and perhaps in full? How many loans does your borrower already have out? Are they responsible with their payments? Does your borrower have a lot of different credit cards? Are these cards paid reliably?

If there is a blip on an otherwise exemplary credit report, ask the person what happened. Did life throw a curveball? This is a person-to-person lending situation, so it is in your best interest to look at the individual and what might have happened beyond his or her control. Maybe they had a hard divorce, a death in the family, or temporary job loss.

Take this into your overall analysis of your borrower's credit worthiness. Break each component down and do your research. It is your money to lend and choosing who you lend it to is crucial in structuring the best lending deal. Use all the tools available to you, which obviously includes a credit report.

For a more detailed presentation on credit visit www.becomingthe-bankbook.com.

Summary

Chapter 8 goes further into detail on credit scores, explaining how credit scores and credit reports are generated and how to use them to determine the creditworthiness of a lender.

Keywords

Credit report: "a detailed breakdown of an individual's credit history prepared by a credit bureau."[52]

Equifax Canada: one of two credit bureaus that operate in Canada.

FICO: a data analytics company that provides credit scores.

Instalment loan: a loan where "you receive a lump sum of money and agree to make equal payments over a fixed term."[53]

Open accounts: "an account which remains to be paid,"[54] and remains open until fully paid.

Revolving credit: an account that "sets a credit limit—a maximum amount you can spend on that account,"[55] such as a credit card.

Revolving loan: "a form of credit issued by a financial institution that provides the borrower with the ability to draw down or withdraw, repay, and withdraw again."[56]

TransUnion Canada: one of two credit bureaus that operate in Canada.

CHAPTER 9: GETTING PAID BACK— EXIT STRATEGIES

How long are you willing to lend out the mortgage you have so carefully arranged? This is critically important, and so often private lenders, even very successful ones, neglect to take this very real question into consideration. Don't make the same mistake. In fact, the sign of a good mortgage broker, and by extension a private lender such as yourself, is the true understanding that a mortgage is not meant to last forever. A seasoned broker will ask the pertinent question at the outset: "Just how long will I be lending out this mortgage for and what provisions have I put in place to ensure all the funds are reimbursed at the end of the mortgage term?"

You need to decide at the outset of your loan one of the most important terms that you can determine.

The Length of Your Loan

There are factors that will enter your decision-making process when determining this mortgage term. Are you loaning funds toward a first mortgage? Are you looking at putting together a loan for a second or even third mortgage? You may even be considering loaning out money toward a bridge loan.

Part of laying the groundwork that I keep circling back to is providing for a clearly articulated **timeline** to end a private lending deal. Be clear, in other words, on your **exit strategy**. Just how will the borrower repay you?

Length will be mainly determined by which mortgage type you are focusing on. As a good rule of thumb, you would never want to loan out money for a bridge longer than a three-month term. Why? Well, a bridge loan is by nature only needed to cover a gap in financing for a borrower. If, however, you are considering loaning out funds to go toward a first mortgage then the length can be longer. I would suggest setting it at no longer than three years.

Here are the specifics on length for each type of loan:

1st mortgages	2 years or less
2nd mortgages	1 year or less
Bridge loans	90 days
Blanket mortgages	Varies as per above

You can always include in your mortgage contract a clause that allows an option to renew after the three-month period. When you are looking at a second and certainly a third mortgage, then one to two years would be the preferred term length in order to ensure your money is paid in full, with substantial interest! Most private lending loans do end up typically being negotiated for a one-year term.

In virtually every area of life we set timelines and self-imposed limits. This is even more the case when it comes to money issues, especially lending out money to others. Take the example of the very wealthy man who has his sights set on his future bride. Yes, we hope that he is thinking that his marriage proposal will result in a happily ever after. He probably is not going into the institution of marriage with the intention of divorcing his bride.

However, it is safe to say that he is likely to want to protect his many assets in the eventuality the marriage does not work out. What is his exit strategy? If he was forward-thinking enough to arrange for a prenuptial agreement and his fiancée agreed to sign it, then this will protect him down the road. If a prenup was not arranged, his exit strategy is divorce and a lengthy court battle.

Unfortunately, I don't think he will come out of this unscathed! His exit strategy is going to cost him! Luckily in the private lending world you will not need to "divorce" your borrowers. The loan has a specific date in which it needs to be paid back. The parting of ways is written into the contract from the outset.

It won't be costly, especially if you have made provisions and asked the right questions at the outset to allow for a seamless and cost-effective exit strategy at the end of the loan period. In fact, you should be prepared to end your relationship with your clients! The timeline for your financial relationship is laid out at the outset of the borrowing process.

This is what you need to ask yourself:

1. How are they going to pay me back?

2. How long do I want to keep this borrower as a borrower?

3. How long do I want to keep this money lent out for?

In other words, when you enter into a private lending commitment there must always be provisions put in place for a relatively fast and inexpensive way out. Keep in mind that you will only be able to force a way out of your loan commitment under certain circumstances—namely, if the loan goes into default in any of the ways that I outlined in the Chapter 7. Also, you can get out if the term of the loan is up and you do not want to renew with your current borrower.

The length of the loan that is negotiated will certainly vary from lender to lender. I personally know private lenders who are very comfortable, for example, lending out money toward a second mortgage at rates as high as 12, 14, or even 18 percent for several years. These lenders are happy with this arrangement and are making substantial returns in interest on the loans. Keep in mind that this works within their comfort margin. Determine your comfort level at the outset.

If you would like to see repayment in a shorter time, be clear of this objective before you negotiate any loan. If you have a need for this money to come back at a specific time, you need to be very sure this can happen. For example, if one of your children is going off to university and you will need to use the money from a RESP. If this is the case, you may only want to invest in very short loans. Ensure you speak to your mortgage professional in detail about this.

Oftentimes, you will be lending money to borrowers who are looking for a quick fix to solve financial issues. These could vary from perhaps consolidation loans to refinance debt or fast money to pay for immediate renovations on their home or maybe second mortgages on their current property. On all of these loans, you can set high interest rates with the potential to make a good profit on your investment whether you decide to loan the money out for a year, five years, and more.

I like to look at private lending as a Band-Aid financial fix opposed to a full triage option. There is a financial wound that needs to be fixed in the short term and immediately. We are not looking for a full medical workup and long-term solution to the borrower's financial health! Think of it as stepping in to provide current pain management not long-term financial care.

If you are lending out money to more than one borrower at a time, keep on top of your borrowers and **clearly outline timelines** for repayment **written in your contract**. This way you can more easily manage your various loans and know when to expect repayment on each one.

Example 1)
We put a second mortgage on an entrepreneur that needed $350,000. He requested a two-year term with an option to renew for one more year at 12 percent. He used the money to inject into his company. This gave him the security the loan would not be called, and he could focus on the growth.

Example 2)
It is very rare, but I had an investor and borrower that wanted a five-year private mortgage. This was set at 7 percent but was based on the RBC

prime rate and could reset annually. This gave security to both the lender and borrower.

Interest Rate Escalation

Take a look at your options to encourage repayment. Maybe you want to put in the contract an interest rate escalation. Perhaps you can include an amortization instead of interest-only as you negotiate a mortgage loan. The point to drive home here is that you are literally in the driver's seat. When borrowers approach you, you can determine their specific financial needs.

You are in the position of devising a financial plan that will help them in the short term. You set the goals and terms of the loan as well as the length that money will be lent out. Ask yourself the questions outlined above as you approach each deal. Carefully negotiate terms with your client that work within your comfort margin. Plan your exit carefully and gracefully as you engineer your mortgage loan.

More often than not, the exit strategy is the term of the loan. The mortgages are normally written for a fixed period of time, but you need to ensure they can repay you. Will the house value change enough for a refinance? If they had a credit issue, will it be fixed by that time? Careful consideration needs to be placed here. By far this is the most important aspect of a mortgage and one most lenders and brokers forget to talk about.

Ask your lending professional this question when they present you a deal. "Sounds like a great investment. What will change to ensure the borrower can pay me out in ___ time?" If they don't immediately answer or have a solution, run away.

You can always call a mortgage and force a sale. However, this is an expensive and painful process and should only be done as a last resort. If you have followed the rules, then capital should be protected, but sometimes the emotional energy is not worth it. I had an investor a few years back tell me the following story.

The investor had lent a second mortgage about eight years previously through another broker. The second mortgage was in a small town that did not have very much appreciation. Eight years after lending the money, the house was worth almost the same amount as the day he lent on it.

The borrower started going into default about five years in on the second mortgage. At this point it was suggested that he should power of sale the home and just sell the property. He would most likely take a small loss on his capital.

He chose to not to do this and proceeded to take over the over house (foreclosure), did a massive number of renovations himself, and then tried to sell it. All of his work did not add any additional value other than what the renovations cost him—he spent $50,000 on renovations only to add $50,000 of value. Again, he was advised to sell it and redeploy the capital in good-performing loans. Since he wanted to now "earn" a return on his work, he over-listed the home, and it did not sell. He ended up trying a rent-to-own deal with a tenant who had poor credit.

Against our advice, this borrower had a sloppy credit file. We knew that he would not repair his credit. Subsequently the tenant started missing payments, and after several attempts at new plans the home is finally going for up for sale. Unfortunately, the result will be the same as if he had sold it eight years ago. He would have just saved a lot of effort and would have earned a healthy return on the money being put in good-performing deals. The lesson here is that you should never be emotionally invested in any one deal. The banks have a saying: "First loss is best loss."

This is why exit planning is so critical. Understand the market and the local real estate. Don't be scared to pick up the phone and call a local realtor. Your blurb could follow roughly like this: "Hi Mr. Smith, I am a private lender. I am thinking of lending in a given area. What can you tell me about the market?"

This is a great way to double-check the appraisal value. Ask the relevant questions. Mortgage professionals have a passion for their area of expertise and knowledge that can serve you well. You can also ask a mortgage broker if prices are increasing in the area the property is located. Don't forget the golden rule of real estate: location, location, location!

So, what should you take away from this chapter? Regardless of what type of loan you end up negotiating, you will have to be very clear when it comes to just how long you want to lend out your funds. Take into consideration the risk level of each loan (first, second, or third mortgage or bridge loan) as well as the integrity of your borrower and their history of paying back loans. In this case, your due diligence when it comes to analyzing their credit history plays a pivotal role!

You might consider allowing for an option for renewal written clearly in your mortgage contract so you can assess at the end of the first mortgage term where you want to go with your funds. Maybe also include that acceleration clause. Do your research, be vigilant, and protect your future investment. It is your money to lend and yours to ultimately protect.

Summary

Chapter 9 discusses setting the length of loan to determine when you will receive a return on investment (ROI). The length of loan should be longer for first mortgages and increasingly shorter for second and third.

Keywords

Interest rate escalation/escalation clause: a "clause in a contract stating that the price of a good or service will increase if a cost increases correspondingly."[57]

Return on Investment (ROI): a measure that directly compares "the amount of return on a particular investment, relative to the investment's cost."[58]

CHAPTER 10: STRUCTURING YOUR MORTGAGES FOR MAXIMUM RETURN

What Questions Are You Asking Yourself?

Just as you are asking questions to yourself concerning other aspects along the process of the private lending deal, so too should you sit down and carefully consider what types of mortgages you want to be involved in. Only you are truly most familiar with what makes you tick. After analyzing what personality traits would be most suitable in a potential borrower, you have to look to yourself to see what type of mortgage loan you are most comfortable negotiating.

If this is your first deal and you just want to test the waters and get your feet wet, maybe you will decide to negotiate a bridge loan with your borrower. The time frame is usually very limited—often up to six months—and therefore you will see your money back in a timely manner. Ask your borrower what their specific needs are for this loan.

Are they in need of the money for a short period of time until the deal closes on their house, and do they have proof that they have the funds to cover the upcoming mortgage? In this instance, monies that you lend out to your borrower will be lent out for a designated period of time and those monies will be back in your hands in short order.

One of the aspects of private lending that appeals to me the most—and I feel is quite a beautiful thing—is that as a private lender you are in a position to decide on the overall structure of your mortgage deals. Furthermore, you have the flexibility to determine whether you want to negotiate different types of deals at the same time. Yes, a bridge loan may appeal to you, but that does not stop you from negotiating perhaps a third mortgage if you aim to charge high interest rates, which opens up the potential for high returns.

This point is an important one and leads us quite nicely into the next section that is a crucial aspect of the private lending process.

Just What Goes into Structuring the Deal?

Now we are really getting into the nuts and bolts of the art of private lending. I have been laying out the building blocks that create a solid foundation for a prospective private lender. By now you are also well trained in what to look for in a potential borrower.

By the same token, the list of questions that will help you negotiate a lucrative private lending deal are well embedded in your head. All of these elements are now going to converge when you become familiar with just how to structure the private lending deal.

Don't worry—it isn't complicated. In fact, all we are going to do is take the elements that we have discussed in detail so far and show you in what order each step is considered when actually negotiating a private lending deal with a potential borrower.

Step 1

In order to structure a deal that is both comprehensive and will ultimately provide a healthy return, I can safely tell you that there are basically seven variables that you will have to analyze. Go to our website, beomingthe-bankbook.com, for a free worksheet on each of the following topics:

1. The interest rate that you will be assigning to each loan

2. The term of the loan itself

3. The maximum loan-to-value (LTV) of the mortgage

4. Determining whether the deal is an interest-only or principal + interest loan

5. Deciding whether the loan is a compound interest loan and what type

6. Deciding on what fees (if any) will be associated with the loan

I can confidently tell you that if you look at each mortgage loan assessing and determining each of these financial aspects, you will have a solid deal moving forward. Look at it as a jigsaw puzzle. Each piece of the puzzle represents a component of the mortgage contract. Without all the necessary pieces, the contract is incomplete. With all the pieces in place—magic! Look at each aspect, ask your list of questions, and then home in on the components that are necessary to successful

Interest Rate

We already talked in length about the "usual" interest rates that you can attach to a particular type of mortgage. Depending on what type of mortgage deal you are considering, you can look at a reliable interest rate that will fall within fairly predictable margins. Another key point to keep in mind is that the interest rate you do choose to assign to any given mortgage loan is not contingent or based on the prime rate. Keep in mind that local markets play a big role here. Rates may vary by state, province, or city.

In fact, private mortgage deals are rarely dictated by the prime rate. This is an added element of flexibility that makes lending out your investments for mortgage loans so attractive to many. Let's recap quickly.

First Mortgage: You will be looking at around a 6 percent to 10 percent interest rate that you can reliably charge with this type of loan. This low to moderate risk loan carries interest rates that are easily manageable for borrowers and will produce reliable returns.

Second Mortgage: With a second mortgage you can now start to look at potentially substantial returns on your investment. It is quite standard practice to charge interest rates starting at 10 percent on this type of loan. Depending on the financial capabilities of a particular borrower, you can set interest rates higher than that. A slightly higher risk-based loan, yes, but a real opportunity to make hefty returns on your initial investment.

Third Mortgage: Once you are contemplating loaning out third mortgages to borrowers, you will be faced with a substantial opportunity to make huge returns on your investment. Interest rates on third mortgages tend to start at 20 percent and can potentially run higher than that. A note of caution: try to keep the term on these high interest loans to a shorter time period to protect your chances of recouping your money.

Mortgage Term

Just as in setting the interest rate, it is ultimately your decision what length (term) that you would like to attach to each loan. While it is generally agreed upon by private lenders that a term of a maximum of three years is the most desirable, the most common term is for one year in private lending. Don't overlook the importance of just how long you want each loan to be lent out.

Set the parameters of the loan at the outset. Make necessary arrangements to recoup your money at a time frame that works for you in your overall portfolio goals. Six months? One year, maybe two? There is no exact science to determine any given loan, with the exception of the bridge loan, which is rarely more than a few months in duration.

In general, in the mortgage industry the terms are as follows:

1. **Short-term loans** are typically six months to a year or less.

2. **Medium-term loans** are one to two years on average.

3. **Long-term loans** represent three-to-five-year or more commitment by both the private lender and the borrower you have entered into a mortgage contract with. These mortgage terms are rare in private lending circles.

It is important to mention that when it comes to the private lending sphere, it is very unusual for the length of term of a loan to exceed three years. Loans with longer than two-year mortgage term lengths are rarely negotiated privately.

When it comes to the length of the mortgage term, there are some funds that are suitable for borrowers depending on whether you are negotiating a short, medium, or long-term loan. A general rule of thumb is that if you are going to be lending out cash then it would be best to do this with a loan of medium-term length of one to two years. You could also consider a short-term loan of up to a year when considering loaning cash for mortgage loans.

If you are going to lend from your registered accounts (RRSPs) then it would be preferable to structure your loan as a medium-term loan, but you can consider a longer-term loan as well. If you are thinking of loaning a home equity line of credit (HELOC), it would be advisable to keep the mortgage term length short term.

I would also like to point out here that the type of mortgage loan you are considering also comes into play when calculating loan terms. Are you going to be lending out a cash mortgage? Perhaps you are considering a registered mortgage loan? Maybe the idea of starting with loaning a HELOC appeals to you. Regardless of what arrangement appeals to you, it would be to your benefit to assign the traditional term that is generally assigned to each mortgage loan type.

As your high school science teacher might have told you, it is advantageous for you to complete your homework and research carefully what loan you are willing to negotiate. If you are confident that the borrower is reliable, then determine the term type you will assign to your loan using these general principles.

Ultimately, the ball is in your court when determining the exact length of each mortgage loan you are negotiating. Remember I am helping to lay out the foundation for you so you will be in the position of building up a first-rate private lending portfolio.

Remember that any higher risk and higher rate loan should be negotiated very carefully, and monies should not be lent out for a long term. Your goal should be to lend out your investment money, set a high interest rate, earn maximum return on that investment, and recoup your funds plus profit in a designated shorter time frame.

Maximum Loan-to-Value

Pay attention. In my experience as a private lender and in any course that I have given on the subject, I have stressed that determining loan-to-value on a given loan you are negotiating privately is crucial. Why? Well, it is simple really. You again have to think like a bank. What did I harp on about in previous chapters?

Banks have mastered the art of lending. Now, they may not be lending out their prize money privately, but they are applying principles that you must incorporate into your overall game plan to be ultimately profitable. Magic formula? Loan out as little money as possible at the highest interest possible for the shortest time frame possible.

Let's break that down and apply it to the concept of loan-to-value. It is important that you have your private lending hat on now and remember you are loaning out money. You are *not* the borrower.

However, when you are lending out your money, your aim should be the opposite. Lend out as little as possible so that you increase your chances of getting all your money back at the end of the mortgage term. In other words, the higher the loan-to-value, the higher the risk. The lower the loan-to-value on the negotiated mortgage, the lower the risk.

Let's define the term that the mortgage industry refers to as loan-to-value. It is important that you are clear on the exact meaning of this term that helps form the basis of decisions that mortgage brokers and lenders use to determine the risk of each particular mortgage loan.

The term represents the ratio of the first mortgage amount of the total appraised value of real property. The equation breaks down as literally loan value (requested mortgage amount) divided by the appraised value (the value of the property in question).

Loan/Value= LTV

The gold standard loan-to-value ratio that the banks and major lenders have generally agreed upon for mortgage loans is 75 to 80 percent loan-to-value. This does not stop you from loaning 90, 95, or even at 100 percent loan-to-value. I would caution you, however, to be very certain that the borrower has the capital, capacity, and collateral to cover a loan, which is such a high loan-to-value. It would be worth your time to watch the video "Why LTV Is Critical When Lending" at becomingthebankbook.com.

Here are some examples of LTV AND LTV guidelines:

Value	1st Mortgage	2nd Mortgage	Loan-to-value (LTV)
$500,000	$250,000	0	50%
$500,000	$250,000	$100,000	70%
$500,000	$100,000	$250,000	70%

Decide on the Interest Type at the Outset

Believe me, I am more than aware there are a considerable number of variables that come to play when you are actually sitting down to structure a mortgage deal. There are also plenty of decisions to be made. As you are shaking your head wondering just how you will bring all these elements into play seamlessly, let me remind you of one important principal: don't put the horse before the cart. Take your time and make sure that all the elements that go into crafting a solid private mortgage deal have been carefully weighed. One step at a time. Look at each variable and structure a deal that ultimately appeals to you as a private lender.

Ask yourself again, "What do you want to achieve as a private lender?" What is your goal? Enough of the pep talk. There is still more to cover when it comes to structuring the deal. Just as there are a number of mortgage types, so are there different types of interest arrangements associated with each mortgage. The ones that I feel are worth mentioning at this point include a principal plus interest mortgage arrangement, a compound interest mortgage, and an interest-only mortgage.

In general, the standard principal plus interest loan is used primarily by the banks based on different mortgage lengths or amortization periods. Be aware that these loans are often difficult to calculate. Your borrower will pay the interest payments that you have assigned to the mortgage amount monthly plus a portion of the principal, or mortgage amount. In this mortgage arrangement the borrower is making interest payments as they slowly pay off the mortgage amount you loaned to them.

This loan is considered a front-loaded loan. The interest is higher at the start of the loan and decreases gradually as payments are made over the term of the loan. Once more of the principal is paid off, the interest earned on the loan is lessened also. When you are deciding what term length would be ideal for a loan that is structured as a principal interest loan, it would make sense to structure this loan as a long-term loan.

An **interest-only loan** is structured exactly as it states. The borrower only pays the interest that you have assigned to the loan and not the principal or loan amount. If you loan out $100,000 and assign a 6 percent interest rate to that mortgage amount, your borrower will be paying the monthly interest payments only on that amount. They will not be paying off any of the $100,000, which represents the principal amount.

What happens to the actual loan amount? Well as you probably guessed, it is not paid off until the end of the term of the loan that you have determined with your borrower. This type of loan is also used often by the big banks, for the most part, for second mortgages or HELOCs. The house is used as collateral in these mortgage arrangements.

In the realm of private lending, interest-only loans are the loan of choice! This stems from the fact that the interest on the loan is spread out evenly. The interest does not decrease over time, as is in the case with the principal plus interest loan. The interest-only loan is always far easier to calculate than the principal plus interest structured loan.

A big bonus too! Why not make your life easier? This is especially relevant when you have lent out funds to more than one borrower at a time. Interest calculations will take less time and it will be far more productive when managing your multiple investments.

Weighing Your Options: What Is in Your Best "Interest"?

Which interest arrangement is best suited for your purposes? What are the advantages and disadvantages of each? We touched upon some of the advantages already. Now let's continue and lay out some of the more obvious pros and cons of both types.

Principal Plus Interest

This interest option is used more commonly for longer-term loans as the interest that is calculated becomes less over time. One could refer to it as a form of front-loaded interest. What I mean by this is that most of the interest that is earned on the principal plus interest loan is paid at the beginning of the loan. As the borrower starts to make inroads into the principal mortgage amount, the interest on that amount becomes less.

As I mentioned earlier, banks tend to structure interest payments this way on the majority of their mortgage loans. Amortization periods vary from 20 to 25 or 30 years. So, this type of loan may be appealing on one level because the loan amount is paid over time. Additionally, you will receive more interest payments at the beginning of the loan. Be wary, however, that ultimately there will be less interest paid out to you as a lender. As a result, that interest is also hard to calculate because it is adjusted as the principal amount is slowly paid off. Unless you have a sophisticated loan system, I would not recommend doing this.

Interest-Only Loan

Let me preface this section on interest-only loans by saying that of the two types of interest arrangements you can attach to a mortgage loan, interest-only is by far the preferred option for private lenders. The main reason is quite obvious. There is simply more interest paid out on this type of loan *and* it is straightforward to calculate! That is a very attractive arrangement if you ask me! If that is not incentive enough the whole loan will be repaid at the end of the term length you have negotiated for your borrower. Furthermore, all the interest payments are spread out evenly.

A Little More on Interest

It is a given that you are investment savvy and that is why you are reading this book cover to cover. You and I know that part of this investment knowledge is being acutely aware that when you are assessing your investments in other investment vehicles, the one variable that you will always be following closely and wanting to earn more of is interest on those hard-working investments.

Really, this is our bread and butter when it comes to investing in any form. By now you are seeing clearly that one of the biggest advantages to the investment strategy of private lending is that there is plenty of opportunity to make even double-digit interest returns on some private mortgage deals.

In order to make such interest decisions and calculations easier, it is important to make a few distinctions at this point. Essentially there are two main types of interest arrangement you will be choosing from when structuring your private loans. **Simple interest** and **compound interest**. With simple interest calculations it is quite forward to determine the interest that you will be earning. In fact, there is simple formula that can be followed:

P: Principal loan amount

I: Interest rate

N: Number of months of the loan

That equation looks like this: **P x I x N**

An example would look like this: $100,000 (P) x 10% (I) x 2 months (N) = $20,000

Although with interest-only loans, it is a very simple method of calculating the interest, the second type of interest, compound interest, is actually the interest type that is far more attractive to private investors and consequently used far more often. What is compound interest? It is literally interest on interest or interest paid on interest.

Yes, compound interest may be more difficult to calculate than simple interest, but you will ultimately be making more money off your investments. You and I know that money talks, so I am fairly confident that you will be using compound interest when it comes time to making crucial decisions in regard to your preferred interest type. If you do choose compound interest it will be handy to keep some truths, or rule of thumb, in mind when it comes to compound interest. It is not rocket science, just a couple of tips to help you navigate.

1. More **frequent compounding** is always preferable when structuring your loans

2. Use **short-term** mortgage length with frequent compounding!

3. **Always calculate APR when using compound interest** or calculating any fees you will be attaching to your loan. This last point is very important because every time you structure your mortgage contract, you must be careful to keep the interest charges within legal limits. Remember any interest over 60 percent is deemed illegal in Canada and is written into law!!

This is VERY important on small loans. In most jurisdictions the total cost of loan is included in calculating this. This includes: legal fees, appraisal fees, lender fees, broker fees, appraisal etc.

A Little More on APR

APR is the annual interest rate. APR is an important element that must factor into your overall decisions regarding both the percentage of interest you will be assigning to your deals and also any fees that you will also decide to charge your borrowers. Top of your mind should always stay legal when determining interest charges and overall fees incumbent on your borrower.

To calculate **APR,** use these variables:

APR Annual Percentage Rate

C: Cost of borrowing (rates, monthly payments, fees, etc.)

T: Term of the mortgage

P: Principal mortgage amount

So, the formula you will be using will look like this:

APR = 100 x C / (T x P)

Consider the following scenarios:

Example 1:
Loan amount: $25,000
Rate: 10%
Term: 1 year
Payments: $208.33
Total cost in the year: $208.33 x 12 = $2,499.96

APR = (100 x $2499.96) / (1x$25,000) = 10%

Makes sense, right? Now let's add a fee of $5,000.

Example 2:
Loan amount: $25,000
Rate: 10%
Term: 1 Year
Payments: $208.33
Total cost in the year: $208.33 x 12 = $2,499.96
Fee: $5,000.00

APR = (100 x $2499.96 + $5000) / (1x$25,000) = 30%!!!! That is a BIG difference.

Now what happens when we this two-year deal?

Example 3:
Loan amount: $25,000
Rate: 10%

Term: 2 years

Payments: $208.33

Total cost in the year: $208.33 x 12 = $2,499.96

Fee $5,000.00

APR = (100 x $2499.96 + $5000) / (2x$25,000) = 15%

By taking the fee over two years, this spreads the APR over both years making it 15 percent.

The point to take away from the inclusion of the APR in your decision-making process when structuring your mortgage loan is that elements such as the term of the loan, the fees you have assigning to your borrower, and the interest rate, plus a possible interest rate premium can bring up the overall interest rate to high levels. **As long as these levels do not exceed what is deemed criminal rates (60 percent or higher),** then the potential for high interest returns is there, especially if we are talking in terms of compounding interest on your loan. Ensure you comply with local laws. It has by my experience that should loans default, judges do not look kindly on lenders that get close to the criminal rate. I have even heard stories of them balking at rates of 8 percent or even 10 percent.

Fees! Interest Is Not the Only Bread and Butter

You might want to hit the gym to clear your head or sit down with a cup of coffee. It's too much to think about, right? No. You are following the formula and examining all the important variables to reach a private lending mix that works for your needs. Feeling better? Okay, let's keep the ball rolling and talk about what fees you will be assigning to your mortgage loans.

When you are structuring your mortgage deal with a borrower, you have looked at the five Cs and have ensured that these criteria have been met. You have determined what financial source you will be using to lend out (RRSP, TFSA, etc.). You have decided the term (length) of the loan as well as what type of mortgage loan (first, second, third, syndicated). You have also decided what interest will be attached to the mortgage loan.

To add to your decision-making process, *never* neglect determining what fees you will be assigning to your loan and make sure you have discussed and written down these fees in the mortgage contract with your borrower.

What Are Some of These Fees?

Banks. You probably have a set of feelings about them ranging from hatred to awe. Your hate probably stems from the amount of money they are making off us and our hard-earned money. Your awe probably stems from how on earth they make such huge profits without many of us even realizing it!

Not many people stop to ask themselves how the banks are making such huge profits. They may grumble about it but not necessarily take the time to analyze just how they are raking it in. Well, if you look at all the accumulated interest they are earning on the legions of different loans they are offering, you can begin to see how the profits may be adding up. But this is not the only money-maker for the big banks. So much of their success can be traced back to the fees they attach to everything from mortgage and student loans to everyday fees on our hard-earned checking accounts!!

Stop and think about this for a moment. If the bank decides to add an extra one dollar in service fees per month to your banking account, it may not seem like a big deal from the perspective of one individual. Now assume that 10 million customers also received an increase of one dollar to their bank fees. Do the math. That is an extra 10 million in profits per month for the bank!

Remember one of the golden rules that will make you profitable in your new career as a private lender. **THINK LIKE THE BANKS.** After structuring your deal, take the time to choose what fees you will be attaching to each private mortgage loan. You can do it. The banks have done it for years!

Before I list some of the fees that you should be considering as a private lender, I must advise you that the fees and interest that you decide to charge **cannot exceed the criminal rate**. In other words, you must protect yourself when determining fees and interest levels. It is advisable to base your fees and interest on the APR. This of course is one of the main reasons why it is of benefit to you to use licensed people when structuring your deals.

Let's get down to the nuts and bolts of what types of fees are associated with private mortgage loans. There are several things that I like to refer to as **upfront fees** that will become standard practice and need to be calculated using the **APR formula**. They should be included **in writing** into your private mortgage contract.

- **Lender Fees**: Charge these for the administrative and processing of your loan. Always outline these fees in the contract you have set up with your borrower.

- **Legal Fees**: Pertaining to any legal involvement in the mortgage contract and all processing fees, which add up quickly! Outline these in your contract with the borrower and articulate they will be responsible for these fees.

- **Broker Fees**: General fees to cover work you have put in on the mortgage contract. Keep track of these fees and list them as they too add up quickly! Make sure your borrower is aware and will take responsibility for these fees.

- **Appraisal Fees**: To cover costs associated with obtaining appraisals on property. It is very important as the appraisal will determine the overall value of the property that you are lending out your investments toward. Your borrower will be responsible also for these fees, so inform them in writing.

- **Percentage or Point Fees**: Another option open to you is charging a percentage of the loan upfront, which is separate from the monthly interest rate that you have determined. This fee can also be referred to as charging points to your borrowers. A reasonable point or percentage fee could be 1 percent, sometimes 2 percent or two points of the loan. This would help you as the lender covers costs setting up the mortgage contract.

A portion of your profit will undoubtedly come from the fees that you assign for each mortgage loan. Don't overlook the importance of researching, calculating, and assigning fees that you see fit with your borrower. Interest rates and fees are your friends. Assign them wisely and start reaping the rewards!

- **Missed payment fees**: Don't overlook writing these fees into your contract as a penalty charges.
- **Insurance Fees**: Make sure that all insurance payments are being made and nothing expires during the course of your loan. Another valuable penalty charge to put in place in your contracts.
- **Annual Administration Fees**: This will cover the costs of maintenance of your self-directed RRSP accounts and set up fees on contracts.
- **Mortgage Prepayment Penalty:** If a mortgage is paid back early, there is often a penalty charged to the borrower unless you specifically did an open mortgage.

Some other fees you could also consider including in your contract would be a purchaser appraisal fee, a preparation of statement fee, discharge fees, and general maintenance fees. You can see how these fees add up and will factor into the overall profits you will be making off your private negotiated mortgage loans.

Summary

Chapter 10 discusses the steps to structuring a deal, taking into account interest rate, mortgage term (short, medium, long), interest type (simple or compound), annual percentage rate (APR), and fees (lender, legal, broker, appraisal, percentage or point, missed payment, insurance, annual administration, mortgage penalty).

Keywords

Annual administration fee: a fee to compensate a lender for costs associated with the administrative processing of a loan on an annual basis.

Annual Percentage Rate (APR): "the yearly interest generated by a sum that's charged to borrowers or paid to investors."[59]

Appraisal fee: a fee that covers costs associated with obtaining appraisals on a property.

Broker fee: a fee to compensate a lender for work they have put into a mortgage contract.

Insurance: "a contract, represented by a policy, in which an individual or entity receives financial protection or reimbursement against losses from an insurance company."[60]

Legal fee: a fee to compensate a lender for costs associated with legal involvement and processing.

Lender fee: a fee to compensate a lender for costs associated with the administrative processing of a loan.

Missed payment fee: a penalty applied when a borrower misses a mortgage or interest payment.

Mortgage prepayment penalty: "a fee that some lenders charge when you pay all or part of your mortgage loan term off early."[61]

Percentage/point fee: a fee charged as a percentage of a loan amount, separate from interest.

CHAPTER 11: THE APPRAISAL—THE FIVE MOST IMPORTANT MINUTES OF YOUR LIFE

Structuring the deal is paramount to your success. I can't stress enough how important the role of research becomes for each mortgage loan you negotiate with a lender. After some practice and time in the private lending sphere, you will begin to recognize key traits to look for in a borrower based on my recommendations. You will know intrinsically what clauses are important for you to include in the mortgage contract. You will know what type of interest arrangement you will make with your borrower, and you will know exactly how to read and pull what is necessary from a credit report.

You will also be very familiar with what fees you want to assign to your deal. The type of mortgage you want to lend out will become clear to you based on your risk tolerance and particular goals. So too will the ability to calculate reasonable interest rates for each mortgage loan.

Moving forward, there is another key to success that will open doors to you in the private lending business. The key to structuring a profitable mortgage loan is based heavily on the **appraisal** of the property in question. This property you are reviewing represents the mannequin that your mortgage deal is hanging on and serves as collateral for your private mortgage loan.

One of the first rules of private lending is to make sure that the house or real estate that you are securing your loan against is up to date in terms of its market value. It is crucial that you know everything there is to know about the property in question before you contemplate lending out money for a second or perhaps third mortgage on that same property.

Remember you are putting your investments toward real estate. Don't leave any stone unturned when finding out everything you need to know about the property in question. Your goal is to get the maximum return on your real estate investment. It stands to reason that being as familiar as you can with it only benefits you while maximizing the odds of a strong return on your private investment in that property.

Know your product. Seek out other properties in the same neighbourhood to see how the property is comparing and holding value. Be thorough with your research. Your guide will be the appraisal. It is best to be familiar with it inside and out. Maybe have two appraisals ordered on the property to see if they stack up. I will provide you with some insight into the often-mystifying appraisal process. You will become best friends with this important real estate document as you build your private lending portfolio.

The Appraisal: The Theory behind It

I am sure that if you have ever contemplated buying a residential property or even thought of dabbling in buying and renting out properties you have heard mortgage professionals throw out the term appraisal more than once. You may have wondered why the realtors and mortgage professionals put so much emphasis on the appraisal when submitting mortgage requests to various lenders. By the same token, why the lenders put so much emphasis on the appraisal when reviewing properties and deciding on whether to lend out financing on these properties.

It is quite straightforward, really. When lenders are deciding to approve mortgage requests on an existing property for a second or maybe even third mortgage, they need to have information on several key issues.

Equity: The property in question is what the lender will be securing any additional loans on. In order to assess how risky such a venture is, the lender is looking to see how much equity is built up in the house already. Remember that you will, as a private lender, be using the property as the primary asset to secure the loan against. Having the question of the amount of equity that has been built up will be of primary importance when assessing whether to help finance the property further. This is why, as we had mentioned earlier, you may consider structuring a blanket mortgage. This will allow you to secure your loan against two properties with the whatever equity is built up in each

Comparable: Having picked up this book, we know that you have an active interest, or at least curiosity pertaining to real estate. This is why I am certain that you are already aware that real estate value is directly related to location, location, location! It boils down to the desirability of the area more than the property itself.

Appraisers will look to other properties in the same neighbourhood or surrounding area to help assess the market value of the property that needs financing. By assessing other similar properties in the same location, appraisers can have more information to go on when determining market value for the property. Of course, there will always be differences between properties that will affect the market value of an individual property.

Consider hiring more than one appraiser to be able to compare any conclusions they come up regarding the property and the ultimate value of the property in question. Any large discrepancy will give you pause for thought. Likewise, similar conclusions on the value of the property will give you the green light to base your contract on the agreed-upon market value.

Maybe the house in question was built the same year as the one right next door. It might even have the exact same floor plan and square footage. This provides the fundamentals for a solid comparable to help assess the overall market value. However, what if there are significant upgrades to the comparable that increases the overall selling price? Renovations will increase value upward and will affect how the appraisers will be assessing the market value of the property in question. Is there a pool in the backyard? Significant landscaping improvements? You get the idea.

How to Choose a Good Appraiser

Of the many things on your to do list when setting up your private lending portfolio, it cannot be stressed enough that you need to put yourself out there and form solid working relationships with reputable appraisers. This is where you should turn to real estate and mortgage professionals to get reliable advice on recommended appraisals in the mortgage field.

Where do you start? Just as in the case of any job that you require professional services for, be it movers for a long haul move or a plumber to fix your sink, make sure that the appraiser you choose is affiliated with a reputable association.

The Appraisal Institute of Canada (AIC) is the professional association of Canadian real estate appraisal professionals. The association currently has over five thousand members across the country. Each province has an affiliated professional provincial association representing recognized and proven appraisers for that particular province. Professional appraisers must meet the minimum professional standards set out by the AIC to be considered highly competent and capable of performing the job for you.

Refer to the list of accredited appraisers in the associated branch of the AIC to secure a reliable appraiser moving forward. Invest in building a positive working relationship with this appraiser. A well-oiled ship sails much smoother, so put in the effort to build trust with an appraiser (or two) to help you with private real estate investments that you will be adding to your overall portfolio.

Simply put, make several of the accredited appraisers your friend! Check out their credentials thoroughly and form a mutually beneficial working relationship with them. You will need their professional expertise as you craft your private mortgage deals. These appraisers will form part of your overall investment team.

It is so important that you have unbiased opinions about the property in question. It is also advisable to have more than one opinion as well. Mortgage professionals are there for you to use as an important resource. An appraiser can also provide you with **useful real estate consulting services** to help you answer any queries you may have. In addition, you can approach your appraiser to **review an existing appraisal** to pinpoint the important features you should be focusing on in the document. An experienced appraiser should be an integral part of your overall investment team.

The Appraisal: What to Look For

During the appraisal process, private lenders are in the same position as other mortgage professionals and are seeking the same key information from the appraisals. What you should be looking for is an accurate and unbiased assessment of the property that you are securing a loan against with your borrower.

Ask the right questions. Be involved in the process. Make sure that the appraiser has explained to you his or her findings. Look at all the variables that might have an impact on the final appraised value of the property. We touched on some of these previously. They would generally include:

1. The year the property was built.

2. The overall condition of the property.

3. Any upgrades and any renovations that may affect the final appraised value.

4. Value of other properties in the same area.

5. State of the electrical, plumbing, roof, etc.

Once again, these variables have value when compared against similar properties within the same area or location.

There are two types of appraisal reports: the **form reports** and the **narrative reports**. A full sample appraisal report can be found in the appendix at the back of the book.

For a form report, the appraiser that you hire will fill out a form that is a general template to be filled out. They will provide all necessary information within this document. Conversely, in the narrative report the information that the appraiser will provide to you is written out, rather than entered onto a standard form. Any reasons or rationale behind the appraiser's decisions will be written out in full.

It is most likely that you will be requiring the form report. Generally, this report type is used with smaller residential properties or small rental properties with no more than four units. At least at the beginning of your new venture into the realm of private lending you will be investing your resources toward smaller residential properties or very uncomplicated and smaller rental properties.

As a result, I would advise you to focus your efforts on securing form appraisals moving forward. Again, if you feel more comfortable, have more than one appraisal made on the property you are reviewing. It is unlikely that you will be required to ask for a narrative appraisal because nine times out of 10 these are used for the purposes of valuing very complex properties and larger constructions.

Key to keep in mind for the best result from the appraisal process you must factor in other considerations. Make sure that the appraiser that you form a working relationship with is fully accredited and affiliated with a major body like the **Appraisal Institute of Canada**. Equally important, make sure you factor in any appraisal fees when calculating your investment.

This next disclaimer stems from what I have been repeatedly saying. Carefully research your appraisers and make sure that you do not have any potential for conflict of interest. Make sure that you have written disclosure from your appraiser that there is no possibility of a conflict of interest when assessing the property in question. At the end of the appraisal process you must ensure that you receive an **appraiser's certification**. Ask for a document that is signed by your appraiser that certifies the appraiser's full acceptance of the appraisal and the contents of the appraisal itself.

At one point you will be so comfortable with the appraisal process and knowledgeable about what to look for that it will be second nature. You will understand the language the appraiser is using, the reasons behind the findings, and the factors that could potentially affect market value. This is related to the homework that goes into each mortgage deal that you put together. Research and understanding go a long away in the private mortgage investing game! Don't blame your elementary school teachers for hammering home the value of homework. This is one area where these skills will pay dividends and more importantly high interest!

The appraisal process is undoubtedly a very crucial component in the private lending process, but it is nothing to fear or shy away from. What you should focus your efforts on is ensuring that you are carefully researching and lining up the best appraiser or appraisers to meet your particular needs. Make sure to ask for all relevant documentation and make sure that safety guards are in place to protect your investment. Tackle every stage of the private lending process with excitement.

Word to the wise: do your prep work and get everything down in writing, from the specifics of the loan you are setting up with your borrower to the appraisal and everything in between. If information pertaining to each loan is clearly laid out and written in your contract there will be no need for backtracking at later stages. You can focus on establishing the conditions to produce sizable returns on your hard-earned investments.

Summary

Chapter 11 discusses what an appraisal is, how it is determined, and why it is a crucial component of any private lending deal as it is a way to determine the market value of a property.

Keywords

Appraisal Institute of Canada (AIC): an accreditation body for appraisal professionals in Canada.

Comparable (comp): buildings "in a specific area that (…) (an individual is) looking to buy or sell in."[62]

Sample first page of an appraisal report. To see the full report, turn to the appendix in the back of the book.

CHAPTER 12: RRSP (AND OTHER REGISTERED ACCOUNTS) MAGIC

As you look around you and try to collect your thoughts about what course to take in this brand-new realm of private lending, stop for a moment and consider what your main source of investment has been up until now and what you feel comfortable doing with this hard-earned money moving forward. The fact that you are turning your attention to the area of real estate investing on a private level shows me that you are more than ready to look at other avenues seriously as a way to relatively safely invest your funds while feeling confident that you will receive consistently high returns.

Don't take offence to what I am about to suggest, but it is entirely possible that you have been a little misguided when it comes to the best route to invest your funds up until now. Banks are quite adept at subtle "brainwashing" when it comes to convincing their patrons to invest only with them and with what portfolio options they may be offering. I emphasize the word subtle because we so routinely turn to the banks without the necessary financial knowledge to counter what they may be suggesting.

Ask yourself who has repeatedly, and may I say quite convincingly, advised you that you should lock in your money in "traditional" forms of investments. Could it be the financial adviser you are paying a pretty penny for to give you "sound" advice? Maybe it is the big bank that is in possession of your checking and savings account and now has advised you to invest in their many varied investment portfolio options? You can begin to see a pattern here.

We are therefore easily guided and persuaded to invest our funds with them. Perhaps mistakenly thinking this is the only safe and reliable route available to us. You may have been investing your money for years in any number of sources and in any number of investment portfolios that have been offered to you by financial advisers and the big banks. Perhaps you have felt very comfortable and "safe" parking your money in sources that you have been told are secure and will provide decent returns for you in the long run.

Yes, these traditional forms of investments are certainly there to be utilized and they do have some advantages. Indeed, this form of investing may represent a more than satisfactory option for some individuals. However, the banks are advising you that you must invest your funds with them for a reason.

The banks also want you to be "scared," or at least intimidated by other options that are available for their own interests. It is no secret that the banks will not receive any commission off your real estate profits. They will not be able to reap the benefits of the many fees that you and I know you can charge your borrowers.

Who wants to make a substantial profit off your investments? Maybe the banks? You know better. You are sharing your returns with the bank, which makes it very difficult to consistently earn decent returns on your investments. Don't get me started on the number of fees, both obvious and sometimes less so, that the banks are charging to park your money LOCKED IN with them.

Instead of the bank collecting the many fees associated with your various investments and a portion of the return, why not set your own terms. Charge your own fees. Invest your money in what type of mortgage you choose and for how long without having a bank determine the overall parameters.

By now you know that there is another area of investing that is not only growing in popularity but has been proven to represent one of the safest and most likely forms of investments to produce high returns consistently. Private lending is a platform that will not let you down. It is also more likely to earn you higher returns over time while still remaining a relatively safe investment option. Remember the golden rule: real estate always appreciates.

What Does the Stock Market Routinely Do?

It can be more than volatile and routinely goes up and down. I like to equate it to a roller coaster. An endless journey at the amusement park is a good analogy. Mind you, some people have very high thresholds. Going up and down may not make them feel sick to their stomach. Seeing the routine dips in the market is not enough to have them biting their nails and gluing themselves to their computer screen watching the stock trends like a hawk.

Others not so much. Instead of riding this often-tense ride, put your money into real estate where you determine the terms and can pull your money out when needed.

There is no such thing as predictable or "normal" rates of annual returns in the stock market. It is just accepted that unpredictability and overall volatility truly describe the nature of the beast. Long-term rates of return may fare a little better. However, are you really willing to invest your funds for such a long period of time in the hopes that you will ultimately profit?

Ultimately, it's your call, but I am here to say that there are other alternatives. Setting your sights on investing your capital in the real estate sector in the form of private lending mortgages to borrowers will not disappoint!

By now you are also familiar that you can lend out any number of your existing investments to offer borrowers loans for different types of mortgages on their properties. Maybe your money is parked in TFSAs, or low-risk mutual funds, or sitting in a high-yield savings account.

It is important to look at your funds as a mechanism to provide the capital for a potentially lucrative mortgage deal. Your funds may be stored in any number of investment channels, but the key to remember is that this capital is what you will lend out to your borrowers at rates that fall within reasonable margins and at terms that seem reasonable for the type of mortgage you have negotiated. Look at all your investment options.

Lending with Registered Accounts: RRSPs, LIRAs, TFSAs, Etc.

For the purposes of this chapter, we will be focusing on how you can invest your RRSP in private mortgage loans, whether it be a first mortgage loan on a property or a second and even third mortgage on an existing property. It is entirely possible that you may not even be aware of the untapped potential there exists in lending out your RRSP investments for the purposes of private lending to potential borrowers.

We are at the point in the book where we must discuss in detail the various vessels or channels in which you can lend out your money. Which one is most preferable? This is a no brainer. I strongly advocate the use of your existing registered investments. Whether it be money invested in TFSAs, money in educational savings plans, LIRAs, or something else. The trick I divulge in this chapter is just what RRSP platform is far more conducive to utilize for the purposes of privately loaning money for real estate mortgages.

It can be argued that analogies are sometimes the best way to look at something new that you may be trying to wrap your head around. I know that I am very guilty of using them when trying to articulate or demonstrate a concept that is unfamiliar. I like to look at it as a visual representation of an often-abstract concept. When we are dealing with the various methods that we can tap into to provide the necessary capital to invest in private mortgages, I can think of a few suitable analogies that would help you visualize the process.

Take the analogy of a house that contains rooms that have different purposes. Let's call it our investment house for our intended purposes. If you look at the method of investment as representing this house, it contains several rooms that are set up as designated areas for different types of investments. It is only now that we can begin to distinguish traditional forms of RRSP investing compared to the form of RRSP investments that I will be advocating.

One room in this investment house is set up as the "traditional" room and therefore is only intended for RRSP investments that are offered by the bank and are locked in. Yes, you could theoretically withdraw funds if needed. However, I am sure that you are aware that any potential withdrawal that you may be considering will come with a hefty withholding tax. These types of investments do carry with them the advantage of providing a tax shelter until they are tapped after 65. Then the government will come calling! They can also be designed to be very low risk if this is your risk tolerance.

The bank will "manage" your portfolio, which can be comforting for some. On the flip side, this leaves you with little or basically no control over the investment strategy and overall course of the investment direction. DON'T FORGET THAT THE BANK IS SHARING SOME OF YOUR PROFIT. The interest you are earning off your investments will be reduced by the interest share the bank is profiting from.

Traditional RRSP investment portfolios can also include any number of different investment options. Maybe yours is made up entirely of low-risk mutual funds. Maybe it includes mutual funds and some more high-risk stocks. The portfolios will vary from investor to investor. Portfolios will depend on the financial advice you have been given by a financial adviser or someone in the bank. They will also undoubtedly reflect your overall risk tolerance. It will also reflect your long-term investment goals and objectives.

There are several common threads that will remain the same regardless of how the actual portfolio is made up:

1. Tax-free investment options.

2. Directed and controlled by the banks and financial advisers.

3. Varying risk levels depending on how you have been advised or what you are comfortable with.

4. Locked in with the potential to withdraw funds with a substantial penalty to consider.

Preferred Option for Private Lending—Self-Directed RRSPs

While I agree that one of the best sources to tap into when considering loaning out money for a private mortgage deal is your RRSP and other registered investments, the actual vehicle that will ultimately be driving your investments should be different from the traditional registered products advocated and directed by the banks and other large financial institutions.

This is where I would like to introduce you to an investment vehicle, or to go back to our analogy, a specialized room in our investment house, that will serve as the engine that fuels your private mortgage lending ventures. This raises important questions that I will draw your attention to at this juncture.

To be in the best position to lend out your funds for privately negotiated mortgages, you really should ask yourself two important questions moving forward:

1. Do you want to have control over your investment portfolio so you can decide the types of investments that you will have the freedom and flexibility to loan out for potentially lucrative private mortgage loans?

2. Do you want to have more control over the interest earned and the power to charge fees to your clients rather than have the bank slowly eat away at your nest egg?

The types of investments—whether they be in your RRSP LIRAs, such as TFSA, low-interest mutual funds or higher interest stock, GICs or bonds—is not the primary concern. You certainly have flexibility to create the portfolio you are comfortable with and keep your existing mix of investment options. **The key is the vehicle or room in the house that you park or move your investments into.** This will provide the ability to loan out money readily for private mortgage loans moving forward with you squarely in the driver's seat.

Direct Your Journey: Travel and Invest with Freedom and Security—Self-Directed RRSP Portfolios

If you were given the option of driving along a busy highway or flying in a plane, which one would you choose? I bet many people would jump up and say driving. This is because we are conditioned to think that driving is safer and more predictable and a standard way of getting to and from one place to another. Just like banks and financial advisers have been telling us for years, similarly conditioning us to stick with registered investment options through their existing channels.

Stop and think about it for a moment. How much control do you really have in a fast-moving vehicle with all the unknown and uncontrollable elements that we face on the highway? What are the weather conditions? Who else is on the road? Are they in a good condition to drive? The point to be hammered home here is that you may think you are directing your vehicle down the freeway, controlling all the variables as you go.

In reality, you have very little control. The banks are in control of your portfolio options. And they are reaping the rewards by sharing in the interest earned. You are not directing the highway or investment traffic moving forward.

Let's take the example of flying to the same destination. The plane has sophisticated navigational equipment and is in constant contact with the traffic control tower from takeoff to landing and every point in between. The pilots are highly trained professionals who are routinely tested to see that they can handle the job in the best professional capacity. And all the other planes have the same advantage and are tracked by traffic control.

Now you may want to rethink which is the better way to travel. By choosing to fly you are directing your safety and have the advantage of securing a much more pleasant and safe scenario. Wouldn't you want to have the same advantages when it comes to investing your funds?

Especially when you want to free up these funds to invest in private mortgage ventures. I think you would rather pilot your own investment portfolio than drive down the traditional banking highway with very little control or ability to direct investment traffic.

You now know the reasons behind it. Now I will tell you which route to navigate to secure your funds while freeing them up to invest privately. Transfer your funds over to the self-directed RRSP account. There, that was not so scary, was it? The funds can still remain in investment options that fit your financial short- and long-term needs.

The big difference between this method of RRSP investments and registered options is that *you* direct your portfolio within the account. *You* monitor and navigate your investments. *You* choose the route. *You* pilot your own investment route and journey.

Just How Do You Go About Setting Up a Self-Directed Account?

1. You are on board with the idea that self-directing your investments not only makes sense but will be fun.

2. You will have the control over the funds and what you do with them in your account.

3. You will be responsible for monitoring and directing these funds.

4. You will be in the advantageous position of deciding what fees are charged and offloading those fees on your borrowers.

5. You will not have to pay commission on the interest earned on your investments to the banks!

6. Now we have to figure out just exactly how to open a self-directed account and put your different funds into this account moving forward.

The good news is that it is a very straightforward process to open a self-directed RRSP account. The only thing to keep in mind is that many of the big banks do not offer the option of clients privately lending mortgages (hint: they will not be profiting from such a method of investments, so they are not making it a readily available investment platform).

That does not mean it will be difficult to set up a self-directed account. You just need to know which financial institutions allow you to proceed easily with privately investing your money for mortgages. The two major institutions that serve as trustees for your RRSP account include:

1. Olympia Trust

2. Canadian Western Trust

You will need to approach either of these financial institutions to open a self-directed RRSP. The process couldn't be simpler. You will only be required to fill out an application form. I am sure you didn't think it would be this straightforward right? Most things in life are far more complicated. Thank goodness for small miracles. What did I tell you? This is the magic of privately investing your money toward mortgages. With the right platform it truly is magical!

You have opened your account and made sure that the application is complete, now you have to put money in this account. You will obviously be either adding new money to your account maybe in cash or in the form of a check. You will also be transferring over other funds from previous investment vehicles.

1. **Cash and checks**: Just go ahead and deposit these funds into your account to reserve for investment purposes.

2. **Transferring funds**: It is more than likely that you have money tied up in other investment vehicles and need to get these funds over to your new self-directed RRSP account. The important distinction to make here is that you will not be withdrawing these funds. This will result in a tax penalty (we are talking about RRSP investments after all). You will, rather, be transferring these funds to your newly set up self-directed RRSP account. Again simple. It will only require filling out a **transfer form**. See? Easy peasy.

Advantages of Self-Directed RRSPs

For the purposes of private lending, this vehicle is ideal for the very reasons I just alluded to. Instead of tying your money up in registered options and essentially giving over control and direction to the bank or financial institution to guide your investments, you take over the steering wheel and drive, or pilot your investments down your chosen investment route.

1. You take over this responsibility of tracking the progress on your chosen investments.

2. These investments are still tax-free investments.

3. You can keep your mix of investment options or choose new options.

4. The risk level remains the same. The difference is that now you can monitor carefully how your chosen investments are faring.

5. There are not very many fees attached to this investment vehicle.

6. When you choose to withdraw money to lend out for a private mortgage loan you can assign some of these fees to your client!

Of all the investment vehicles that are available, it is no secret that I am advocating you set up a self-directed RRSP account for our purposes. Private lending is perfectly suited to utilize funds from this account. By accessing funds in self-directed accounts, you retain control over the direction of these funds and how you are going to allocate them. As a private lender it is vital that you have this flexibility and that you are on top of how your investments are faring.

This becomes especially important when you are lending out more than one mortgage loan at a time. Having multiple real estate investments forces you to know exactly how your funds are doing while allowing you the freedom to loan out at different times to potential lenders.

Other Advantages Include:

1. **Allows for the centralization of your investments**: Being organized and having a central mechanism, or investment hub, in which to

loan out private mortgages is much more efficient and will provide for seamless tracking of your mortgage investments.

2. **You can more easily administer the RRSP account**: With multiple investments held in your RRSP account, including funds for lending out for private mortgages, this account is ideal because all the administration is linked to this one account. This makes it far easier to handle any administrative issues pertaining to your investments in one investment platform.

3. **Investment consolidation**: If you keep your investments in multiple platforms, it becomes quite difficult to monitor and retain a sense of how your investments are working for you. When you are in the position of privately loaning out mortgages, it is far more beneficial to have all the funds under one account to provide for a solid business plan.

4. **Investment selection**: Now you may be very happy with the investments that you have selected up until now. This is fine. Transferring them over to a self-directed RRSP account will be straightforward. However, this would be a good time to look at your existing investments as well as maybe looking at other investment options that would be an ideal vehicle for lending out privately. The point to be made is that with transferring over your investment portfolio to a self-directed RRSP account you can add other investments and easily transfer others. Flexibility is the key. Control in deciding your investment direction is also key.

5. **Choose different companies to invest in**: It is possible that up until now you have been advised to invest most of your funds in one company that has been recommended as a company that you can profit from. It may be time to look at other companies. With a self-directed RRSP account, you can choose to research different companies anddiversify a bit if you feel there exists other options that are suitable for your investment purposes.

Private lending requires discipline. There are so many aspects that we have touched upon that need to be factored in and accounted for. This is why it is crucial that you set up and maintain a centralized method to track all your private investments. Like so many pursuits in life, organization is key.

Consolidating administrative tasks, investments, and being able to track your progress is vital. At one point you will have more than one mortgage loan that you are loaning out. When ensuring that each mortgage loan is working for you, it is imperative that you have this central hub in which to maintain control over your investments moving forward.

You are firmly behind the steering wheel when it comes to privately lending out funds for private mortgages. With self-directed RRSP accounts you will not need to rely on a GPS. You have the navigational guide. You can control the elements that lead you forward on your investment journey toward being a successful private lender. Steer your private lending career in the direction that is most comfortable for you.

Summary

Chapter 12 outlines the opportunities available when lending via registered accounts such as RRSPs, TFSAs, and LIRAs. A self-directed RRSP, in particular, has huge advantages; it is still a tax-free fund, but taking control of choosing and monitoring your investments allows for greater returns.

Keywords

Locked-in Retirement Account (LIRA): "a type of registered pension fund in Canada that does not permit withdrawals before retirement except in exceptional circumstances."[63]

CHAPTER 13: **A LITTLE BIT ON THE LEGALITIES**

I f I could emphasize one thing it would be to make sure all of your protections are firmly in place before you consider loaning out your funds
for a private mortgage. It is not that I am inferring that private lending out
funds for mortgages is an inherently risky venture. By now you know that
comparatively, it is one of the safest forms of investment options available
today.

Rather, when you do negotiate your mortgage contracts with borrowers, it is imperative that both parties are aware of the legalities involved.
Make sure that all your legal protections are outlined clearly *in writing*.
Equally important is that you should have a very competent real estate lawyer involved in the mortgage process. Make sure to hire a very competent
real estate lawyer to be established as part of your mortgage team.

Research and understand what you are legally responsible for. Research
and be clear on what legal aspects fall under the responsibility of your
borrower as well. This particular section of the book is not lengthy by any
means. In this instance quantity, is not the issue. Substance becomes the
main thing.

You must be aware of any legal aspects pertaining to mortgage deals
that you structure now as well as any you enter into down the road. I think
the best way to tackle this important element to the private mortgage process is to outline in point form the legal aspects that will be your respon-

sibility to cover. Equally important, don't forget that your borrower is on the hook for different legal aspects pertaining to the mortgage contract that you have worked out together.

Is It Legal? Mortgage Legalities to Be Aware Of

Let's list the legal aspects that you will need to be thoroughly aware of moving forward. Some of these legal points will fall under your list of responsibilities while others will be up to the borrower to be aware of. These are basically legal generalities. The more you are prepared, the better the results. Another golden rule that has ruled my work ethic from my early days in this business.

Relax. This is all part of properly carrying out your background preparation on each private mortgage deal that you commit to. Research and be aware. Knowledge is power. You do not want to be caught in a situation where you are unclear of your legal responsibilities as well as that of your borrower.

1. Make sure that you work with an established real estate lawyer to help draft your mortgage contact and go over all the legal aspects pertaining to your mortgage contact. Have this lawyer as part of your investment team.

2. Make sure you take the provincial rules for dealing with mortgage default under consideration before taking any steps in the default process (see Chapter 6).

3. Make sure you and your real estate lawyer include a clause in your contract of power of sale in case you are faced with the unlikely scenario of borrower default.

4. Make sure you carefully go over each clause with your borrower and inform them what they are legally responsible for.

5. When finding borrowers, make sure to only advertise on online local classifieds or other sites with specific details. Otherwise, you may be found to be advertising illegally without a mortgage licence.

6. Be careful to set interest rates at levels that cannot be deemed to be set at a potentially "illegal level."

7. There is no governing body that regulates the activities of private lenders. Having said this, it is imperative to set interest rates that are fair and reflect somewhat the market standard. Also, you must follow provincial guidelines pertaining to default rules.

8. If you do choose to liquidate your assets in an RRSP account to put those funds in a new self-directed RRSP account, make sure you are aware of any tax penalties you may be responsible for. This is why it is recommended to transfer over these funds.

9. Make sure there are no existing leans on the property you are using as collateral for your mortgage loan. This becomes a legal issue to resolve before taking on your borrower.

Most of what I am recapping has been outlined in detail in previous chapters. It is important that you keep these legal generalities in your mind as you progress as a private lender. As there is not currently a government body that encompasses private lenders, the onus is on you to be aware of legal issues that may arise, or to at least be aware of, when you structure your private lending deals.

Summary

Chapter 13 emphasizes the importance of legal counsel to protect you in your private lending deals. You must be aware of local laws, tax implications, and setting your interest rates within a legal range.

CONCLUSION: BE THE MASTER OF YOUR JOURNEY

One of the greatest experiences we can have in life is being fortunate enough to be able to embark on a new journey providing us the opportunity to explore a new area of life that has not been on our radar for whatever reason. Maybe this represents a new endeavour that you have been wanting to dive into. Sometimes it represents a trip that allows us to step out of what we are familiar with and encompass new experiences and perspectives.

We have done just that in this book. Together, we have taken a curiosity, interest, or even strong desire to embark on the journey that is the realm of private lending. We have entered this new investment territory and explored every pertinent aspect that is relevant to you when you contemplate becoming a private lender. This is an exciting process. There is so much to learn and encompass when directing your efforts toward this fascinating and potentially lucrative area of investing.

Real estate is such an exciting sector with such untapped potential. Mortgages, in particular, are both complex and interesting. The mortgage industry is constantly evolving and provides an endless backdrop of investment opportunities. I don't want you to miss out on these opportunities.

In fact, I want you to truly embrace these opportunities and take full advantage of this lucrative and exciting area of private investment.

We have hammered home many times throughout our journey together about the importance of **asking the right questions** through each step of the private lending process. This point is probably the biggest takeaway from the book.

Questions pertaining to **who** you want to lend your funds out to. Just **how** you want your funds to be lent out. Choosing **which interest arrangement** you will opt for. For just **how long** your mortgage term will be. Questions pertaining to whether to proceed with **compounding interest or interest-only loans**. Also, **what fees** to charge your borrowers. **What method** to use when handling the unlikely case of default. And how to determine the **credit worthiness of your borrower**.

Put that private lender's hat on. Wear it with confidence. Step up to the plate. Take control of your investments. Remember that the two key advantages of private lending out your funds toward different types of mortgages are that it will provide you both **control** and **flexibility**.

Don't let the banks determine the terms of your investments. You now know better! Don't let the banks charge you commission and many assorted fees. Use this control that private lending your funds provides. You are a lender now. You are in charge of what fees you will charge and how many!

Use the magic of loaning out your funds from a self-directed RRSP and you can say goodbye to the traditional restraints that other forms of investments invariably have. You are the master of your own journey. You are literally steering your financial ship and driving your investments in the direction that you have determined.

Enjoy the journey. Enjoy the control. Enjoy the freedom. Above all else, take the direction and tips you have been given and have fun in your journey toward becoming a private lender. It was a pleasure!

APPENDIX: APPRAISAL REPORT

RESIDENTIAL APPRAISAL REPORT

Joe & Associates Ltd.

REFERENCE:

FILE NO.: 2222-3333

CLIENT

CLIENT: Great Lender Inc.
ATTENTION:
ADDRESS:
E-MAIL:
PHONE: FAX:

APPRAISER

AIC MEMBER: Joe Appraiser
COMPANY: Joe & Associates Ltd.
ADDRESS: 20 Anywhere Street
Smalltown, ON X1Y 2Z2
E-MAIL: Joe@joe.com
PHONE: 613 333-4444   FAX: 613 333-4455

SUBJECT

PROPERTY ADDRESS: 11 Anywhere Drive   CITY: Smalltown   PROVINCE: ON   POSTAL CODE: X1Y 2D2
LEGAL DESCRIPTION: Lot 385, Plan 111111.

Source: MPAC / Geowarehouse

MUNICIPALITY AND DISTRICT: City of Smalltown
ASSESSMENT: Land $ Imps $ Total $ 380,000   Assessment Date: January 1, 2021   Taxes $ 4,853   Year: 2021
EXISTING USE: Residential Single Family   OCCUPIED BY: Owner

ASSIGNMENT

NAME: Dan Homeowner   Name Type: Owner
PURPOSE: [X] To estimate market value [ ] To estimate market rent
INTENDED USE: [ ] First mortgage financing only [X] Second mortgage financing only [ ] Conventional [X] Financing not to exceed 80% loan to value ratio.
INTENDED USERS (by name): Great Lender Inc.
REQUESTED BY: [ ] Client above [X] Other Mortgage Agent
VALUE: [X] Current [ ] Retrospective [ ] Prospective
[ ] Update of original report completed on   with an effective date of   File No.
PROPERTY RIGHTS APPRAISED: [X] Fee Simple [ ] Leasehold [ ] Condominium/Strata
MAINTENANCE FEE (if applicable): $
CONDO/STRATA COMPLEX NAME (if applicable):
IS THE SUBJECT A FRACTIONAL INTEREST, PHYSICAL SEGMENT OR PARTIAL HOLDING? [X] No [ ] Yes (if yes, see comments)
APPROACHES USED: [X] DIRECT COMPARISON APPROACH [X] COST APPROACH [ ] INCOME APPROACH
EXTRAORDINARY ASSUMPTIONS & LIMITING CONDITIONS [ ] NO [X] YES (see attached addendum)
HYPOTHETICAL CONDITIONS [X] NO [ ] YES (see attached addendum. A hypothetical condition requires an extraordinary assumption)
JURISDICTIONAL EXCEPTION [X] NO [ ] YES (see attached addendum)

NEIGHBOURHOOD

NATURE OF DISTRICT: [X] Residential [ ] Commercial [ ] Industrial [ ] Agricultural
TYPE OF DISTRICT: [ ] Urban [X] Suburban [ ] Rural [ ] Recreational   AGE RANGE OF PROPERTIES (years): New   From New   To 10+/-
TREND OF DISTRICT: [ ] Improving [X] Stable [ ] Transition [ ] Deteriorating   PRICE RANGE OF PROPERTIES: $ 400,000 $ 800,000+
BUILT-UP: [X] Over 75% [ ] 25 - 75% [ ] Under 25% [ ] Rural   Steady market demand
CONFORMITY Age: [ ] Newer [X] Similar [ ] Older   MARKET OVERVIEW: Supply: [ ] High [X] Average [ ] Low
Condition: [ ] Superior [X] Similar [ ] Inferior   Demand: [ ] High [X] Average [ ] Low
Size: [ ] Larger [X] Similar [ ] Smaller   PRICE TRENDS: [ ] Increasing [X] Stable [ ] Declining
COMMENTS: [ ] Detrimental Conditions Observed

Value trends, market appeal, proximity to employment and amenities, anticipated public/private improvements, apparent detrimental conditions (railroad tracks, unkempt properties, major traffic arteries, hydro facilities, commercial/industrial sites, landfill sites)

The subject neighbourhood is located 26 miles west of downtown Smalltow just west of Ridge Street and east of Any Avenue. The area is developed with a mixture of 1 and 2 storey single family and semi-detached residences. The neighbourhood has good access to all amenities including major traffic routes, shopping, and schools. The immediate area is a new, developing subdivision known as "The Glen". No adverse influences noted.

SITE

SITE DIMENSIONS: 28.67' X 117.5'   UTILITIES: [X] Telephone [X] Natural Gas [X] Storm Sewer [X] Sanitary Sewer [ ] Septic
LOT SIZE: 3800   Unit of Measurement Sq.Ft.   [ ] Open Ditch [ ] Holding Tank
Source: MPAC / Geowarehouse   WATER SUPPLY: [X] Municipal [ ] Private Well
TOPOGRAPHY: Sloping slightly from dwelling to rear lot line

FEATURES: [ ] Gravel Road [X] Paved Road [ ] Lane [X] Sidewalk [X] Curbs
CONFIGURATION: Generally Rectangular   [X] Street Lights [X] Cablevision
ELECTRICAL: [ ] Overhead [X] Underground
ZONING: R2-42 - Residential   DRIVEWAY: [X] Private [ ] Mutual [ ] None [X] Single [ ] Double
Source: City of Smalltown   [ ] Underground [ ] Laneway
OTHER LAND USE CONTROLS (see comments):   Surface: Asphalt
USE CONFORMS: [X] YES [ ] NO (see comments)   PARKING: [X] Garage [ ] Carport [X] Driveway [ ] Street
ASSEMBLAGE: [X] NO [ ] YES (see comments)   LANDSCAPING: [ ] Good [X] Average [ ] Fair [ ] Poor
TITLE SEARCHED: [ ] YES [X] NO (see comments and limiting conditions)   CURB APPEAL: [ ] Good [X] Average [ ] Fair [ ] Poor
COMMENTS: [ ] Detrimental Conditions Observed

Include features such as zoning, official community plans, local area plans, flood plains, EPA, greenbelt, reserves, heritage, easements, site restrictions such as judgments or liens, assemblage, known documentation of environmental contamination, tanks, etc.

The subject site is situated on Anywhere Drive just south of Any Woods Drive and north of Prince Street. The site backs onto open space area and a lake. The generally rectangular shaped site has 28.67 feet of road frontage, a site depth of 117.5 feet and is improved with a detached 2 storey dwelling circa 2019, together with a 1 car built-in garage. A single paved driveway accesses the site, dwelling and garage. Grounds are landscaped with lawns and shrubs. The rear yard is enclosed in wood fencing and there is a deck off the rear of the dwelling. No major adverse influences noted.

Form produced using ACI software. 800.234.8727 www.aciweb.com
Appraisal Institute of Canada © Ottawa, Canada 2018
Page 1 of 5
AIC Ful 09/18
AICFULL_0818 11192018

Joe & Associates Ltd.

RESIDENTIAL APPRAISAL REPORT

Joe & Associates Ltd.

REFERENCE:

FILE NO. 2222-3333

YEAR BUILT (estimated): 2019	PROPERTY TYPE: Single Family Dwelling Detached	ROOFING: Asphalt Shingles	
YEAR OF ADDITIONS: n/a	DESIGN/STYLE: 2 Storey	Condition: [X] Good [ ] Average [ ] Fair [ ] Poor	
EFFECTIVE AGE: 2+/- years	CONSTRUCTION: Wood Frame	n/a	
REM. ECONOMIC LIFE: 58+/- years	WINDOWS: PVC Thermal Glazed		
COMMENTS:	BASEMENT: Full	EXTERIOR FINISH: Stone and Vinyl Siding	
N/A	ESTIMATED BASEMENT AREA: 893 [X] Sq. Ft. [ ] Sq. M.	Condition: [X] Good [ ] Average [ ] Fair [ ] Poor	
	ESTIMATED BASEMENT FINISH: 0 %	n/a	
	FOUNDATION WALLS: Poured Concrete		

BEDROOMS(#)	BATHROOMS(#)		INTERIOR FINISH	Walls	Ceilings	CLOSET:	[ ] Good [X] Average [ ] Fair [ ] Poor/None
1 Large	1	2-piece X	Good	[X]	[X]	INSULATION:	[X] Ceiling [X] Walls [X] Basement [ ] Crawl Space
3 Average		3-piece	Average	[ ]	[ ]	Info Source: Inspection / Assumed	
Small	2	4-piece	Fair	[ ]	[ ]	PLUMBING LINES: Pex, ABS	Info Source: Inspection
		5-piece	Paneling	[ ]	[ ]	FLOOR PLAN: [ ] Good [X] Average [ ] Fair [ ] Poor	
		Poor		[ ]	[ ]	BUILT-IN/EXTRA: [ ] Stove [ ] Oven [X] Dishwasher [ ] Garburator	
FLOORING: Ceramic, Laminate, Carpet						[ ] Vacuum [ ] Security System [X] Fireplace [ ] Skylight [ ] Solarium	
ELECTRICAL: [ ] Fuses [X] Breakers						[X] HR Ventilator [X] Central Air [ ] Air Cleaner [ ] Sauna [ ] Jetted Tub	
ESTIMATED RATED CAPACITY OF MAIN PANEL: 200 amps						[X] Garage Opener [ ] Swimming Pool	
HEATING SYSTEM: Forced Air Fuel type: Gas							
WATER HEATER: Type: Hot Water On Demand						OVERALL INT. COND: [X] Good [ ] Average [ ] Fair [ ] Poor	

ROOM ALLOCATION

LEVEL	ENTRANCE	LIVING	DINING	KITCHEN	FAMILY	BEDROOMS	DEN	FULL BATH	PART BATH	LAUNDRY	Utility	Mud	Storage	ROOM TOTAL	AREA
MAIN	X	1	Open	1					1	X		1		3	899
SECOND						4		2						4	1,084
THIRD															
ABOVE GRADE TOTALS ROOMS 7				BEDROOMS 4		BATHROOMS: 2F 1H								7	1,983
BASEMENT										1		1		2	893

UNIT OF MEASUREMENT: [X] Sq. Ft. [ ] Sq. M.

SOURCE OF MEASUREMENT: Measured

BASEMENT FINISH: The full basement is unfinished and houses the dwellings utility and storage space. Perimeter insulation.

GARAGES/CARPORT/PARKING FACILITIES: 1 car built-in garage.

SITE IMPROVEMENTS (INCLUDING DECKS, PATIOS, OUTBUILDINGS, LANDSCAPING, etc): Deck, covered front porch, fencing and maintained grounds.

COMMENTS: [ ] Detrimental Conditions Observed [ ] Incomplete Construction (see comments)

Building, appearance, quality, condition, services, extras, personal property, etc.
The subject site is improved with a 2 storey detached dwelling known as the "Sylish" model and was constructed by Arthur Homes, a reputable local builder. The exterior is clad in stone and vinyl siding, the roof is asphalt shingles and the windows are PVC thermal glazed units. Heat is provided via a gas furnace, the dwelling has central air, an HRV system and the electrical service is 200 amp on breakers. Functional floor plan and average/good overall aesthetic appeal. Flooring is a mix of laminate, carpet, and ceramic. The main level is developed with a front foyer, a 2-piece washroom, laundry/mud room with garage access, kitchen with a centre island and rear deck walkout and an adjoining open living/dining area with gas fireplace. The second level is developed with a 4-piece bathroom and four bedrooms including a large primary suite with a walk-in closet and 4-piece ensuite bathroom with double vanity and walk-in shower.

Form produced using ACI software. 800.234.8727 www.aciweb.com
Appraisal Institute of Canada © Ottawa, Canada 2010
Page 2 of 5

AIC Full 05/16
AICFULL_05/16 11109549

Joe & Associates Ltd.

159

RESIDENTIAL APPRAISAL REPORT

Joe & Associates Ltd.

FILE NO.: 2222-3333

REFERENCE:

LAND VALUE AS IF VACANT: ☐ N/A $ 150,000   SOURCE OF DATA: Manual, Contractor, Files   Comment: N/A

HIGHEST AND BEST USE

EXISTING USE: Residential Single Family

HIGHEST AND BEST USE OF THE LAND AS IF VACANT: ☒ Residential ☐ Other

HIGHEST AND BEST USE OF THE PROPERTY AS IMPROVED: ☒ Existing Residential Use ☐ Other

ANALYSES AND COMMENTS: The subject is a legal and conforming land use under the current zoning bylaw, and it conforms well with neighbouring properties.

DIRECT COMPARISON APPROACH

	SUBJECT	COMPARABLE NO. 1		COMPARABLE NO. 2		COMPARABLE NO. 3	
		Description	$ Adjustment	Description	$ Adjustment	Description	$ Adjustment
	11 Anywhere Drive	123 Fake Drive		132 Fake Street		145 Fake Bay	
	Smalltown	Smalltown		Smalltown		Smalltown	
DATA SOURCE		MLS#1234		MLS#12345		MLS#123456	
DATE OF SALE		22-Jun-2021		12-May-2021		29-May-2021	
SALE PRICE	$	$ 705,000		$ 680,900		$ 749,900	
DAYS ON MARKET		5		1		27	
LOCATION	Horizon Dr./Greenspace	Similar/Inferior	10,000	Similar/Inferior	10,000	Similar/Inferior	10,000
SITE DIMENSIONS/LOT SIZE	28.67' x 117.5'	32.8' x 105'		35.6' x 97' (Corner Pie)		37.2' x 100' (Corner Irreg.)	
BUILDING TYPE	Detached	Detached		Detached		Detached	
DESIGN/STYLE	2 Storey	2 Storey		2 Storey		2 Storey	
AGE/CONDITION	2 : Good	3 : Good		2 : Good		2+/- : Good	
LIVABLE FLOOR AREA	1983 Sq.Ft.	2125 Sq.Ft.+/-	-9,000	1462 Sq.Ft.	31,000	2400 Sq.Ft.	-25,000
ROOM COUNT	Total Rooms 7 : Bdrms 4	Total Rooms 7 : Bdrms 4		Total Rooms 5 : Bdrms 3		Total Rooms 7 : Bdrms 4	
BATHROOMS	2F 1H	3F 1H	-4,000	2F 1H		3F 1H	-4,000
BASEMENT	Full/Unfinished	Full/Part Finished	-10,000	Full/Fin/W.Out	-25,000	Full/Finished	-20,000
PARKING FACILITIES	1 Car Built-In	1 Car Built-In		1 Car Built-In		1.5 Car Built-In	-3,000
Extras	AC, HRV, Deck, etc.	Similar		Inferior	10,000	Similar	
Upgrades	Avg.	Similar		Similar		Superior	-10,000
ADJUSTMENTS (Gross%, Net%, Dollar)		4.7% % -1.8% % $	13,000	11.2% % 3.8% % $	26,000	9.6% % -6.9% % $	52,000
ADJUSTED VALUES		$	692,000	$	706,900	$	697,900

ANALYSES AND COMMENTS:

Include qualitative or quantitative explanation for sale conditions, expenditures, market conditions and property adjustments including location, physical/economic characteristics, use, non-realty, rationale for most appropriate comparables.

The sales selected in the Direct Comparison Approach are considered to be the most relevant to the subject valuation at this time. Market conditions in and around the subject area have remained generally stable for the past 2 months and thus no adjustment for time is considered necessary.

All sales are newly constructed detached dwellings situated in and around the general subject area. All sales have superior basement development. All sales are situated on inferior lots not backing onto open/green space.

Sale 1 is a larger dwelling and has an additional full bathroom.
Sale 2 is a smaller dwelling with inferior extra features.
Sale 3 is larger dwelling with an additional full bathroom, superior garage development and superior upgraded features.

After lump sum adjustments the Sales indicate a value range for the subject by the Direct Comparison Approach of from $692,000 to $706,900, say $700,000, which is close to both the mean and the median of the established range.

ESTIMATED VALUE BY THE DIRECT COMPARISON APPROACH   (rounded) $ 700,000

Form produced using ACI software, 800.234.8727 www.aciweb.com
Appraisal Institute of Canada © Ottawa, Canada 2019
Page 3 of 5
AIC Full 05/18
A/CFULL_0518 11193019

Joe & Associates Ltd.

160

Endnotes

1   Adam Barone, "Asset," Investopedia, updated February 28, 2021, https://www.investopedia.com/terms/a/asset.asp.

2   Jake Frankenfield, "Cryptocurrency," Investopedia, updated October 30, 2021, https://www.investopedia.com/terms/c/cryptocurrency.asp.

3   Jason Fernando, "Debt-Service Coverage Ratio," Investopedia, October 4, 2021, https://www.investopedia.com/terms/d/dscr.asp.

4   James Chen, "Actual Owner," Investopedia, January 18, 2021, https://www.investopedia.com/terms/a/actual-owner.asp

5   Kimberly Amadeo, "What Are Emerging Markets?" The Balance, updated October 25, 2021, https://www.thebalance.com/what-are-emerging-markets-3305927.

6   "Equity," Cambridge Dictionary, accessed October 14, 2021, https://dictionary.cambridge.org/us/dictionary/english/equity.

7   Jason Fernando, "Futures," Investopedia, October 5, 2021, https://www.investopedia.com/terms/f/futures.asp.

8   Justin Pritchard, "What is a Hard Money Loan?" The Balance, November 8, 2021, https://www.thebalance.com/hard-money-basics-315413.

9   "Hedge fund," Investopedia, September 4, 2021, https://www.investopedia.com/terms/h/hedgefund.asp.

10   Daniel Kurt, "A Guide for Home Equity Loans and HELOCs," Investopedia, September 11, 2021, https://www.investopedia.com/mortgage/heloc/.

11   Kate Ashford and John Schmidt, "What Is An IPO?" Forbes, updated August 25, 2021, https://www.forbes.com/advisor/investing/initial-public-offering-what-is-an-ipo/.

12   "Joint venture," Cornell Law School Legal Information Institute, accessed October 14, 2021, https://www.law.cornell.edu/wex/joint_venture.

13   Julia Kagan, "Loan," Investopedia, updated April 19, 2021, https://www.investopedia.com/terms/l/loan.asp.

14   Adam Hayes, "Loan-to-Value (LTV) Ratio," Investopedia, updated October 6, 2020, https://www.investopedia.com/terms/l/loantovalue.asp.

15   Adam Hayes, "Expense Ratio," Investopedia, updated July 1, 2021, https://www.investopedia.com/terms/e/expenseratio.asp.

16   Julia Kagan, "What Is a Mortgage?" Investopedia, updated September 8, 2021, https://www.investopedia.com/terms/m/mortgage.asp.

17   "Mutual funds," U.S. Securities and Exchange Commission, accessed October 14, 2021, https://www.investor.gov/introduction-investing/investing-basics/investment-products/mutual-funds-and-exchange-traded-1.

18   Carey Chesney, "Construction Loans: Everything You Need to Know," Rocket Mortgage, November 9, 2021, https://www.rocketmortgage.com/learn/construction-loans.

19   James Chen, "Options," Investopedia, updated September 8, 2021, https://www.investopedia.com/terms/o/option.asp.

20   Chris B. Murphy, "Penny Stock," Investopedia, updated January 28, 2021, https://www.investopedia.com/terms/p/pennystock.asp.

21   Than Merrill, "Ultimate Private Lending Guide: How to Get Started," Fortune Builders, accessed October 14, 2021, https://www.fortunebuilders.com/becoming-private-money-lender-part-1/.

22   Julia Kagan, "Registered Retirement Savings Plan," Investopedia, updated April 24, 2021, https://www.investopedia.com/terms/r/rrsp.asp.

23   Julia Kagan, "Retirement Income Fund (RIF)," Investopedia, updated February 23, 2021, https://www.investopedia.com/terms/r/retirement-income-fund.asp.

24   James Chen, "Risk" Investopedia, updated October 6, 2020, https://www.investopedia.com/terms/r/risk.asp.

25   "Tax-Free Savings Account (TFSA), Guide for Individuals," Canada Revenue Agency, accessed October 14, 2021, https://www.canada.ca/en/revenue-agency/services/forms-publications/publications/rc4466/tax-free-savings-account-tfsa-guide-individuals.html#P44_1110.

26   "security," Merriam-Webster, accessed October 14, 2021, https://www.merriam-webster.com/dictionary/security.

27   Julia Kagan, "Self-Directed RRSP," Investopedia, updated November 30, 2020, https://www.investopedia.com/terms/s/selfdirectedrrsp.asp.

28   Adam Hayes, "Stock," Investopedia, updated May 22, 2021, https://www.investopedia.com/terms/s/stock.asp.

29   "Exit planning," Divestopedia, accessed October 14, 2021, https://www.divestopedia.com/definition/4593/exit-planning.

30   Will Kenton, "Fee," Investopedia, updated June 13, 2021, https://www.investopedia.com/terms/f/fee.asp.

31   Caroline Banton, "Interest rate," Investopedia, updated September 1, 2021, https://www.investopedia.com/terms/i/interestrate.asp.

32   Jason Fernando, "Opportunity Cost," Investopedia, updated October 29, 2021, https://www.investopedia.com/terms/o/opportunitycost.asp.

33   Jason Fernando, "Compound Interest," Investopedia, updated February 16, 2021, https://www.investopedia.com/terms/c/compoundinterest.asp.

34   "Credit Report and Score Basics," Financial Consumer Agency for Canada, accessed October 14, 2021, https://www.canada.ca/en/financial-consumer-agency/services/credit-reports-score/credit-report-score-basics.html.

35   Adam Hayes, "Risk/Reward Ratio Definition," Investopedia, updated December 28, 2020, https://www.investopedia.com/terms/r/riskrewardratio.asp.

36   Will Kenton, "Appraisal," Investopedia, updated November 13, 2021, https://www.investopedia.com/terms/a/appraisal.asp.

37   Julia Kagan, "Blanket Mortgage," Investopedia, updated September 18, 2021, https://www.investopedia.com/terms/b/blanket_mortgage.asp.

38   Troy Segal, "5 C's of Credit," Investopedia, updated September 20, 2021, https://www.investopedia.com/terms/f/five-c-credit.asp#2-capacity.

39   "Capital," Merriam-Webster, accessed October 14, 2021, https://www.merriam-webster.com/

dictionary/capital.

40   "Collateral," Merriam-Webster, accessed October 14, 2021, https://www.merriam-webster.com/dictionary/collateral.

41   James Chen, "Collateral," Investopedia, updated November 27, 2020, https://www.investopedia.com/terms/m/multiple-listing-service-mls.asp.

42   Julia Kagan, "Bridge Loan," Investopedia, updated on May 28, 2020, https://www.investopedia.com/terms/b/bridgeloan.asp.

43   Julia Kagan, "First Mortgage," Investopedia, updated November 27, 2020, https://www.investopedia.com/terms/f/first_mortgage.asp.

44   Julia Kagan, "Second Mortgage," Investopedia, updated on July 31, 2021, https://www.investopedia.com/terms/s/secondmortgage.asp.

45   Bobby Kofman and Sean Zweig, "What is a Syndicated Mortgage and is it a Safe Investment?" KSV Advisory, accessed October 15, 2021, https://www.ksvadvisory.com/docs/default-source/default-document-library/what-is-a-syndicated-mortgage-and-is-it-a-safe-investment-by-bobby-kofman-and-sean-zweig.pdf?sfvrsn=df3957d5_0.

46   Steven Tulman, "Is it too risky to have a third mortgage?" Clover Mortgage, January 20, 2021, https://clovermortgage.ca/blog/it-too-risky-have-third-mortgage/.

47   "Number of Residential Mortgages in Arrears: Month Ended March 31, 2021," Canadian Brokers Association, DB50 Public, accessed June 16, 2021, https://cba.ca/Assets/CBA/Documents/Files/Article%20Category/PDF/stat_mortgage_en.pdf.

48   James Chen, "Default," Investopedia, updated February 17, 2021, https://www.investopedia.com/terms/d/default2.asp.

49   Minda Crace, "Mortgage Default: What It Is, How To Avoid It and What To Do If Your Home is On The Line," Rocket Mortgage, November 20, 2021, https://www.rocketmortgage.com/learn/mortgage-default.

50   James Chen, "Foreclosure," Investopedia, updated November 19, 2021, https://www.investopedia.com/terms/f/foreclosure.asp.

51   James Chen, "Power of Sale," Investopedia, updated July 27, 2020, https://www.investopedia.com/terms/p/power-of-sale.asp.

52   Alexandra Twin, "Credit Report," Investopedia, updated April 7, 2021, https://www.investopedia.com/terms/c/creditreport.asp.

53   "Quick Guide to Instalment Loans in Canada," Spring Financial, July 9, 2021, https://www.springfinancial.ca/blog/loans/ultimate-guide-to-installment-loans-in-canada.

54   "Open Account Definition," The Strategic CFO, accessed October 14, 2021, https://strategiccfo.com/open-account-definition/.

55   Karen Axelton, "Understanding Revolving Credit," Experian, November 11, 2019, https://www.experian.com/blogs/ask-experian/what-is-revolving-credit/.

56   Julia Kagan, "Revolving Loan Facility," Investopedia, updated February 12, 2021, https://www.investopedia.com/terms/r/revolving-loan-facility.asp.

57   "Escalation clause," The Free Dictionary, accessed October 14, 2021, https://financial-dictionary.thefreedictionary.com/escalation+clause.

58   Jason Fernando, "Return on Investment (ROI)," Investopedia, updated September 13, 2021, https://www.investopedia.com/terms/r/returnoninvestment.asp.

59   Jason Fernando, "Annual Percentage Rate," Investopedia, updated September 19, 2021, https://www.investopedia.com/terms/a/apr.asp.

60   Julia Kagan, "Insurance," Investopedia, updated October 12, 2021, https://www.investopedia.com/terms/i/insurance.asp.

61   "Prepayment Penalty: What It Is And How To Avoid It," Rocket Mortgage, October 26, 2021, https://www.rocketmortgage.com/learn/prepayment-penalty.

62   Carey Chesney, "Real Estate Comps: What They Are And How To Find Them In Your Area," Rocket Mortgage, February 24, 2021, https://www.rocketmortgage.com/learn/real-estate-comps.

63   Julia Kagan, "Locked-in Retirement Account," Investopedia, updated January 31, 2021, https://www.investopedia.com/terms/l/locked-in-retirement-account.asp.

Acknowledgments

This book is based upon years on years of lending money and working in the mortgage industry. I would like to acknowledge all the hard work of the lawyers, appraisers, lenders, and clerks. These are the quiet workforce that often only hear when things go wrong. Without their expertise, lending would not be possible. A special thank you to Karen Sucra for her contribution.

LET'S KEEP THE CONVERSATION ─ GOING ─

For in-depth discussions and podcast episodes focused on topics introduced in the book, check out my website.
becomingthebankbook.ca

For **special discounts** or bulk purchases, contact us at **book@becomingthebankbook.ca**

Let's continue the conversation! Join us at...
▶ **The Practical Broker**

CONNECT WITH OUR COMMUNITY

▶ **The Practical Broker**

🎙 **The Practical Broker**

f @Becomingthebankbook

in /ottawachadrobinson

THANK YOU FOR READING!

If *Becoming the Bank* was helpful, please leave a review on Goodreads or on the retailer site where you purchased this book and help me reach more readers like you!

www.ingramcontent.com/pod-product-compliance
Lightning Source LLC
Chambersburg PA
CBHW071232210326
41597CB00016B/2014